D1122370
1pint

Artisan drinks

Lindy Wildsmith

Artisan drinks

Delicious alcoholic and soft drinks to make at home

Photography by Kevin Summers

QUARRY

Quarry Books
100 Cummings Center, Suite 406L
Beverly, MA 01915

quarrybooks.com • quarryspoon.com

For Rafe

First published in the United States of America in 2014 by Quarry Books, a member of Quarto Publishing Group USA Inc
100 Cummings Center
Suite 406-L, Beverly
Massachusetts 01915-6101
Telephone: (978) 282-9590
Fax: (978) 283-2742
www.quarrybooks.com

Visit www.QuarrySPOON.com and help us celebrate food and culture one spoonful at a time!

First published in the United Kingdom in 2014 by Jacqui Small LLP
An imprint of Aurum Press
74–77 White Lion Street
London N1 9PF

10 9 8 7 6 5 4 3 2 1

ISBN: 978-1-59253-994-9

Publisher: Jacqui Small
Managing Editor: Lydia Halliday
Designer: Maggie Town
Editors: Hilary Lumsden, Susanna Forbes
Production: Maeve Healy

Printed in China

Contents

Introduction

I can reach back into my childhood memories to the days when my father used to take me to visit his old aunts and their friends living along the deep country lanes on the borders of Herefordshire and Gloucestershire in England. I have a vague image of a stone cottage nestling at the end of a garden path, shaded by cherry trees and entered by a low, wooden door. Inside was a narrow, draughty hallway, a ticking, chiming grandmother clock, heavy curtains, dark furniture, and a sideboard that offered precious bottles of homemade drinks in welcome: dandelion beer for me, parsnip wine for Dad.

Since then there has been a surge of cheap, mass-produced, convenience beverages: tea bags, carbonated drinks, sugary sodas, concentrated juices, cheap wine and beer, hard cider that has barely seen an apple, and sickly sweet perry (pear cider), but the pendulum has already swung the other way again. We have learned to mistrust mass-produced drinks and have fallen back in love with produce that evokes the past. Enter the artisan producer supplying farm shops, delis, and even supermarkets up and down the country with craft-made drinks, just like Old Mother Haywood or Old Man George down the road used to make.

Yet however lovingly made an artisan product may be, it is never going to be as good—and certainly not as rewarding—as the one you make yourself. If, like me, you love the passing of the seasons and everything they bring, what better way to celebrate them than by making your own teas, cordials, carbonated drinks, cider, beer, wine, and liqueurs? These are guaranteed to be well-crafted, clean, authentic drinks that retain the integrity of the ingredients with which they are made.

Any small step to use what we find on our doorstep, to make the most of nature's harvest, is a step in the right direction. More importantly, it will put us back in touch with the seasons and a steadier and more rewarding pace of life. Traditional culinary crafts are the very essence of slow food, so what better way to spend some time than by making your own artisan drinks?

Conserving the scents, savors, and flavors that nature has to offer is not difficult. There are certain rules and guidelines, but just like with most things, it is experience that counts; the more involved we become, the more experience we gain. We know what we like, and one of the joys of making our own drinks is that through a hands-on approach and trial and error we forge a system that suits us. What's more, the produce we make ourselves is unique—just the way we like it.

Artisan Drinks opens with the "Still Waters Run Deep" chapter, and its vibrant cordials and syrups move on to peppy "Family Fizz." As the book progresses, the drinks get steadily stronger, from "A Global Resurgence" of beer, cider, and perry and "A Very Good Year" of wines to the rich, delicious liqueurs in the "And Now for Something Stronger" chapter. There follows a celebration of traditional and modern punches and party drinks in "Taking the Plunge", while "Happy Hours" is filled with mocktails and cocktails made with the recipes included in this book. To close, an "Oasis of Calm" comforts with teas, tisanes, and spicy brews.

Inspiration There is room for immense creativity, innovation, and experimentation in making cordials and liqueurs—using fruit, flowers, leaves, and spices with impressive results—and there is an array of recipes to choose from. I make no apology for leading you astray, but both crafts are totally addictive. The realm of the tisane and herbal tea is similarly fascinating,

Once upon a time

The crafts of the stillroom were, until the early part of the 20th century, second nature to most householders. So much so that many old family recipes were not even written down, and when they were, there was simply a list of ingredients and little explanation of what to do. Our forbears knew how to make preserves and drinks like we know how to unscrew a jar or take the cork out of a bottle.

particularly when it comes to foraging for leaves, berries, hips, flowers, and seeds to dry and blend to make your very own brews.

Making wines with vegetables as well as fruit and flowers is inspiring, too, but winemaking can be hit-and-miss. From the most experienced amateur to the professional winemaker, all will experience good and bad years, but perhaps this challenge is what attracts people to winemaking. Craft cider- and perry-making are narrow disciplines, in as much as cider and perry can only be made from apples or pears. But they require knowledge and expertise, so I have consulted and quoted renowned English cider-maker Tom Oliver and adhered to the traditions of England's Three Counties (Gloucestershire, Herefordshire, and Worcestershire). Not forgetting the subtleties of international styles, I also look to Normandy, France and the Northeast and -west of the United States. When it comes to beer I have simply set out the first tentative but guaranteed steps towards home brewing.

Creating these drinks is a pursuit that gets under your skin, and once you have acquired the necessary skills you'll find that you want to make more and more; before you know it, you'll have amassed a wealth of expertise. There is the pleasure of the outdoors, of becoming intimate with the seasons and the plants, fruits, and flowers that grow around you; the pleasures of searching, finding, picking, and conserving them to enjoy all winter long; the pleasures of giving them as gifts, sharing them with friends and family, and the simple and wholesome pleasures of drinking them, plus the satisfaction of knowing you made them yourself.

Good health and happiness!

Sourcing & seasonality

If you're interested in food and drinks, you probably already look beyond the supermarket and take time to search your local produce fairs, farmers' markets, and other food-oriented events. These are the places you will find fruit and vegetables as they come into season. What's more, much of it will have been grown in and around the towns and areas in which you live, and will bring with it the true taste of the land.

The anticipation of the arrival of the first season's local gooseberries and the more prosaic plums, for example, is so exciting that I, for one, am more than happy to stay with them while they run their seasonal course and then forget about them for the rest of the year. Who wants that quintessentially summer fruit, the strawberry, all year long? Why do we want to eat asparagus 12 months of the year? Imports have their place; where would we be without foods we don't grow ourselves and all the exotic tropical produce such as bananas and pineapples that we take for granted? Seasonal fruit and vegetables are at their best when they are in season, and because there is generally an excess at the height of the season, they are also at their cheapest: the optimum time to start making drinks.

By preserving fruit and vegetables we prolong the seasons and we turn them into something else: something unique that becomes associated with another time of the year, whether it's a summer drink, an autumn treat, a winter brew, or a festive potion.

The answer lies in the soil Gardening is one of those things you either love or hate—but whatever you think, it is undeniably good for the soul, good for the mind, and good for the body (but possibly not for the back). And it is the ideal way to provide an endless supply of produce to make into drinks.

A kitchen garden brings with it the wonders of producing your own vegetables and fruit. It is a tricky business getting the balance right, and however careful you are about sowing, inevitably at certain moments during the growing season there will be an excess—and this is where preserving comes into its own.

You don't need a large space to create a vegetable garden; in fact, you don't need a dedicated space at all because you can plant fruit bushes and trees and enjoy the blossom in and around flower beds. Wildflowers seed themselves around the garden, and herbs love to grow in pots and baskets; certain vegetables and salads can be nurtured in buckets, bags, or sacks, or distributed around borders to great effect. I have a niece who has an asparagus patch right in the middle of a sunny flower border; it provides a supply of asparagus for weeks on end. The possibilities are endless.

When you grow your own food, you get into the habit of eating with the seasons and making the most of what you have. A fruit tree is the place to start; a plum, damson, crab apple, pear, or cherry tree in your backyard is a triple delight. In spring you can enjoy the clouds of blossom; in summer, the shade it brings; in autumn, the fruit-laden tree. So much fruit that, after you have had your fill for eating, making cordials, liqueurs, fruit juice, and other drinks, there will still be fruit left over to fall to the ground for making wine.

There will be times when it feels like you are eating the same produce over and over again. When the harvest becomes so great, *Artisan Drinks* shows you how to make something to drink for later in the year.

As welcome as the flowers in May Sometime in February each year, the curtains of winter start to draw back and Mother Nature, with her cast of thousands, puts on a show that is quite simply the greatest one on earth; primroses, violets, dandelions, nettles, and countless other edible flowers and leaves file a merry dance, one after the other, through our woods and across our fields from early spring into summer. Blossoming trees and bushes offer a similar show: the sloe and the cherry plum, the pear and the apple, followed by the sweet elderflower, broom, blackberry, gorse, and dog rose. These provide flowers in spring and summer for making sparkling and still wines and cordials, and berries, hips, and fruit in autumn for wines, liqueurs, teas, and more.

Country roads, lanes, and hiking trails, hedges, riverbanks, and woods, and urban parks, squares, riversides, and vacant lots are all rich places for gathering ingredients. It is not enough to go out once and expect to find edible treasures; you need to get to know your hunting grounds and then you'll start to see new things popping up according to the time of year—so always, always walk with a bag tucked in your pocket to gather what you find. But always remember to use a map, never trespass, and only wander across legally accessible land, respecting the laws of all national parks and forests—nature reserves aren't just an open house to all. After all, would you want a complete stranger walking through your own backyard?

The artisan drink-maker's year

Spring

- nettles
- rhubarb
- elderflower
- gooseberries
- green walnuts
- thyme
- dandelion flowers & leaves
- clover flowers
- may blossom (hawthorn)

Summer

- cherries
- strawberries
- currants: black, red & white
- raspberries
- apricots
- nectarines
- peaches
- loganberries
- mulberries
- roses
- lavender
- mint
- rosemary
- fennel flowers

Autumn

- plums
- damsons
- blackberries
- elderberries
- rowan berries
- figs
- grapes
- parsnips
- carrots
- sweet potatoes
- beets
- pears
- quinces
- apples
- hawthorn berries (haws)
- sloes
- rosehips

Winter

- cranberries
- grapefruit
- clementines
- mandarin oranges
- tangerines
- pomegranates
- ginger root
- dried fruits
- oranges
- lemons
- limes

Still waters run deep

Cordials, syrups & soft drinks

Cordials, syrups & soft drinks

In England, the words "lemon barley water" (a homemade cordial) conjure up thoughts of summer picnics, punting on the river, afternoon tea on the lawn, and tennis and cricket matches. Beyond such quintessentially British pastimes, homemade cordials are also useful partners to cakes, desserts, and cocktails, adding color, sweetness and flavor as needed.

Today when we speak of "cordials" and "waters," we mean soft drinks, but a look through an early cookbook tells a different story. In *The Compleat Housewife*, the first cookbook published in the American colonies in 1742, Eliza Smith dedicates a whole section to "All sorts of cordial waters." It debuts with the "Great Palsey Water," which lists half a page of herbs, flowers, roots, and spices as ingredients, starting with:

"Take of sage, rosemary, and betony-flowers, of each a handful; borage and bugloss-flowers, of each a handful; of lily of the valley and cowslip flowers, of each four or five handfuls; steep these in the best *sack*..."

After being steeped, distilled, and steeped again, the resultant "water" promised a half-page of cures:

"... taken inwardly or bathed outwardly it taketh away giddiness of the head, and helpeth hearing; it makes a pleasant breath, it is good in the beginning of dropsies; none can sufficiently express the virtues of this water...."

In the past, huge quantities were made at a time to use up what was available and what was in season, but I prefer to make small quantities.

A spoonful of medicine Smith also includes recipes for "Orange or Lemon Water:" "To the outer rind of an hundred oranges or lemons, put three gallons of brandy and two quarts of *sack*." The orange water was recommended for stomach problems, while the lemon water was known as "fine entertaining water."

There is also the useful "gripe water" for colicky babies, made with pennyroyal, aniseed, coriander, sweet fennel, and caraway seeds—and brandy. Saffron cordial contained marigold flowers, saffron, and *sack* (white fortified wine) or muscadine, a wine made from native wild grapes in the southern United States.

One thing's for sure: our cordials and waters started out as tonics or medicines, containing *sack* or spirits, and were often distilled even more. It should, of course, be remembered that in the past, water was unsafe to drink and even children drank weak ale in its place. These days, homemade drinks such as Lemon Barley Water, Rosehip Syrup, and Elderflower Cordial offer a degree of those medicinal qualities, as well as being refreshing and reviving.

Family fun Cordials are simple to make and the whole family can take part. In fact, traditionally the children were sent out to pick the fruit, flowers, plants, and hips from the fields and hedges. But be warned: even in those far-off days children were paid for their efforts, albeit pennies, and may still demand that today!

Keeping & storage Where you keep your cordials can be as important as how you make them. Natural yeast levels vary depending on which fruit or flower you are dealing with, which season you're in, and even from day to day, depending on the weather. They say a hot, dry summer can mean that yeast levels appear high and are difficult to keep control of naturally.

Equipment

Making cordials does not call for complicated equipment. These basic cooking utensils provide the bulk of what you'll need.

- Large and small bowls
- Clean cloths and clothespins
- Saucepans, large and small
- Large measuring cup
- Medium-sized funnel
- Fine strainer
- Potato peeler and masher
- Brewer's sterilizing solution
- Bottles with good-fitting tops

All cordials are best put into glass, but plastic (PET) can be used. If you plan to pasteurize your cordials, you will need strong, heatproof glass bottles or jars used for preserving (see box, opposite).

You may need

- Food mill, such as a Mouli-legume
- Cheesecloth, muslin, or jelly bag (see page 21)
- Citric acid and tartaric acid
- Food scales, digital if possible

Pasteurization

It is essential to pasteurize cordials, fresh fruit juices, other nonalcoholic and certain alcoholic drinks to keep them unrefrigerated in the long term. The best method is to pasteurize the liquid once it is in the bottle. To do this, fill the sterilized glass bottles as directed, put the sterilized tops on but do not close tightly (see Sterilization box, below).

Use a very deep saucepan or an electric water boiler. Place a cloth or trivet in the bottom, put the bottles in, and add enough water to come just past the level of the liquid inside the bottle. Turn on the heat and hang a thermometer over the side of the pan. Bring the water up to 158°F and hold there for 20 minutes. Take out the bottles, seal tightly, and leave to cool on their sides to ensure that the inside of the cap is sterilized. Store in the dark.

This is the commercial gold standard for pasteurization in order to preserve flavor and color. If you increase the temperature, the flavor will spoil.

Over the years I have noted that sometimes cordials keep well while others start going moldy on the surface after a month or so. So always keep your fruit cordials in the refrigerator, or a cold pantry or cellar.

It is hard to say how long a cordial will keep. I could say three months, but often they soldier on for a year and more. In preparation for this book I made cordials with every fruit as it came into season. I kept a close eye on them all. On some, I noticed a degree of fermentation with a light fizz or telltale bubble appearing, while others remained still.

This may well have been due to the unusually warm summer or a whole raft of other reasons: bottles not being sealed correctly in the first place, the use of recycled bottle tops, poor sterilization, or simply not boiling the fruit long enough. Do take care, therefore, and don't cut corners.

If your cordial does show signs of beginning to ferment within a day or so of being made, reboil the cordial, rebottle (in sterile bottles), and store in the refrigerator, or pasteurize it (see box, above).

Keeping it natural You could use additives but I prefer not to—let's keep things natural wherever possible. When you next open the bottle and look at your cordial, if it retains its bright color and clarity and smells good, it will be fine. Taste a little and if it still tastes good, it's fine.

If a small ring of mold has appeared on the surface, lift it off with the point of a sharp knife or pour it away, just as you would if you found a little mold on the top of jam; after all, sugar is a natural preservative. Again, take a sip to test.

The addition of lemon zest balances a cordial's sweetness and also helps to preserve it. Citric acid can be used instead of lemon zest, or as well as. While adding spices adds depth of flavor and also helps to preserve the cordial, adding spirits such as brandy or whiskey helps preserve it even longer and creates a warming, if potent drink.

Sterilization

It is advisable when making cordials to sterilize not only the bottles but also any equipment used for bottling them, particularly if you plan to keep the cordial for any length of time. Sterilizing powder can be bought either in tubs or as tablets, as used to sterilize baby bottles. Either way, make the sterilizing solution and soak utensils as directed before rinsing in hot water. Or put glass bottles and utensils in a dishwasher.

Makes 1 pint

5 unwaxed limes

1 cup water

1 lb 2 oz granulated sugar

You will also need

2 x 8 fl oz sterilized bottles with stoppers (see box, page 13)

** siroppo is the traditional spelling of sciroppo, as used by Pellegrino Artusi in his book La Scienza in Cucina e l'Arte di Mangiare Bene*

Italian lime siroppo* (syrup)

First recorded in a Medici cookbook of 1696, this recipe was brought to modern times by Pellegrino Artusi, the father of Italian cooking as we know it today. In *La Scienza in Cucina e l'Arte di Mangiare Bene* (*The Science of Cooking and the Art of Eating Well*), he describes this syrup as "excellent and refreshing; however, sadly lacking in cafés in some parts of Italy."

Use a potato peeler to zest 2 of the limes, taking care to avoid the pith. Put the zest in a medium-sized saucepan, add the water, and bring to a boil over low heat. Take off the heat, add the sugar, and leave to dissolve, stirring constantly (*see pic* 1).

Meanwhile, cut away and discard the zest and pith of the 3 remaining limes. Cut away the pith from the 2 zested limes. Using a small, sharp knife, carefully cut out the fruit segments, discarding the seeds and the membrane (*see pic* 2). Reserve any juice that may fall from the fruit.

When all the sugar has dissolved, strain the liquid into a bowl and discard the lime zest (*see pic* 3). Pour the liquid into a pan, add the lime segments and any reserved juice (*see pic* 4), and bring to a boil gently to reduce. Take care not to reduce too much—about 15 minutes at most—otherwise the syrup will caramelize. The liquid is ready when it starts to look syrupy. Pour into a bottle and seal. When required, dilute with ice water to taste.

Making & keeping: Make when citrus fruit is plentiful. Will last 12 months if kept in the refrigerator, otherwise use straight away or pasteurize (see box, page 13).

Variation: The ultimate thirst-quencher, it can also be made with 3 large oranges or lemons, or 2 grapefruit.

Opposite: From left, Syrop de Grenadine (see page 20), Ginger Cordial (see page 21) and Florida Cocktail Cordial

Florida cocktail cordial

This is a delicate cordial made with the zest and juice of oranges and grapefruit. You can use the basic recipe to make a cordial with any mixture of citrus fruit, or with just one type. Like all citrus drinks, it is reviving and thirst-quenching, especially when served over ice with slices of fresh fruit. This is an excellent ingredient for making mocktails (see page 170) and as a base for sorbets.

Makes 1 quart

Thinly pared zest of 1 grapefruit (pink or regular) and 1 orange (blush or regular)

Juice of 2 or 3 grapefruit and 2 or 3 oranges

About 2 cups water

1 lb 2 oz superfine sugar

You will also need

Citrus squeezer

2 x 1 pint (16 fl oz) bottle, or a selection of small sterilized bottles, preferably glass, to give as gifts, with screw- or swing-caps (see box, page 13)

Put the orange and grapefruit zest in a medium-sized saucepan. Add the water and sugar, place over low heat, and bring slowly to a boil, stirring to dissolve the sugar (*see pic* 1).

Juice 2 oranges and 2 grapefruit into a measuring jug. You should have around 2 cups of juice. Juice more fruit if necessary. Add this to the pan (*see pic* 2). Bring back to simmering point and simmer for 10 minutes.

Using a fine strainer, strain the liquid into a measuring jug and leave to cool. Rinse out the sterile bottles and funnel with warm water and fill the bottles with the cordial, leaving a small gap of ¾ inch between the top of the liquid and the top of the bottle (*see pic* 3). Seal.

Making & keeping: Make all year, whenever citrus fruits are at their best. Keep in the refrigerator for a month or so or pasteurize (see box, page 13).

3

Syrop de grenadine

Makes 10 fl oz or 1¼ cups

2 pomegranates

2¼ cups granulated sugar

Strained juice of 1 lemon

1 tsp citric acid

You will also need

Food mill or Mouli-legume

1 x 10 fl oz bottle, or a selection of small sterilized bottles to give as gifts, with screw- or swing-caps (see box, page 13)

This glistening pomegranate "jewel syrup" is a magical must-have ingredient for cocktails, soft drinks, fruit salads, and sorbets. It's a pain to remove the pith from the pomegranate seeds, but the result is well worth the effort.

Cut off the crown (the jagged part at the top of the fruit) and discard. Cut the pomegranate in half from tip down and then in half again across. Scoop out the seeds ("jewels") into a large bowl, making sure to pick out the pith and discard.

Add the sugar to the bowl, crush lightly with the back of a wooden spoon, cover with a cloth, and leave overnight to steep.

The following morning pass through a food mill into a saucepan. Put the saucepan over low heat, stirring occasionally until all the sugar has dissolved. Add the strained lemon juice and the citric acid and simmer for a few minutes.

Transfer to a measuring jug. Rinse out the sterile bottles and funnel with warm water and fill with the cordial, leaving a small gap of ¾ inch between the top of the liquid and the top of the bottle. Seal.

Making & keeping: Make in the autumn or winter. Keep in the refrigerator for up to a year or pasteurize (see box, page 13).

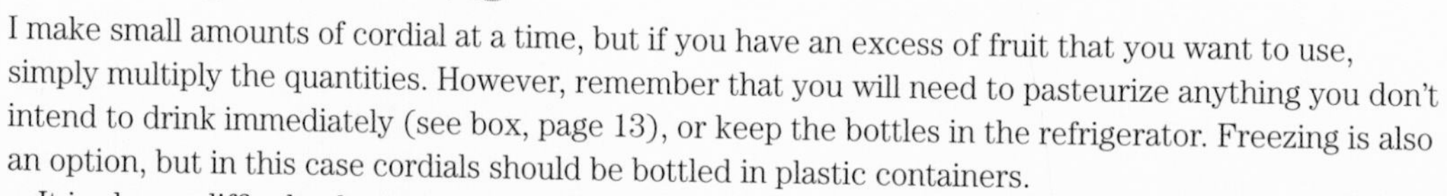

Bottles & quantities

I make small amounts of cordial at a time, but if you have an excess of fruit that you want to use, simply multiply the quantities. However, remember that you will need to pasteurize anything you don't intend to drink immediately (see box, page 13), or keep the bottles in the refrigerator. Freezing is also an option, but in this case cordials should be bottled in plastic containers.

It is always difficult when making drinks or preserves to predict exactly how much a recipe will yield. Quantities vary according to the amount of juice in the fruit, the level of evaporation, and so forth. It is therefore always useful to have a selection of different-sized bottles available.

I rarely make large quantities and thus I have a selection of varying bottles, including 1 pint (16 fl oz), 8 fl oz, and 4 fl oz. These tiny ones are useful for using up small, leftover quantities after filling larger bottles, as well as for giving as presents. When you want to keep your cordial it is important always to fill bottles to within ¾ inch of the cap. Instead of leaving a bigger space, top up bottles with a little boiled water.

Previous pages: Syrop de Grenadine ingredients (left) and Ginger Cordial ingredients

Fine strainer vs jelly bag 

When making cordials it is often sufficient to use a fine strainer to strain them. However, to obtain a crystal-clear syrup it is best to use a jelly bag (*see pic* 2, page 27). There are two types available; the first is an inexpensive version made with synthetic fibers with four loops on the top to hook onto whatever you're using to suspend your fruit and liquid mix from. The second is made with a sturdy cotton fabric and has a stiff collar and strings with which to hang it. Both are suitable, but the cotton bag drips more slowly, producing the clearer syrup.

When using the cotton jelly bag, scald it first by running boiling water through it before adding the syrup. This has the double effect of sterilizing the bag and helping the juice flow freely through the cloth instead of being absorbed by the fabric. Whichever method you use, it is important not to press the fruit but to leave the juices to drain by themselves.

Ginger cordial

Makes 1 pint

7 oz root ginger, scrubbed

Thinly pared zest of 1 lemon

1½ cups turbinado sugar

1¼ cups cold water

Strained juice of 2 lemons and 1 orange

You will also need

Grater

1 x 1 pint (16 fl oz) bottle, or a selection of small sterilized bottles, preferably glass, to give as gifts, with screw- or swing-caps (see box, page 13)

Ginger cordial is an uplifting and warming drink served hot in winter, and a reviving refresher served on ice in summer. It is also the most useful ingredient in the mocktail dispensary as it adds depth of flavor and a mighty kick to a nonalcoholic drink (see pages 172, 178).

Roughly grate the ginger into a large bowl—there's no need to peel. Add the lemon zest, sugar, and water and stir well. Cover with a clean cloth and leave to steep overnight, stirring again in the morning.

Transfer to a large saucepan, put on low heat, and bring slowly to a boil, stirring occasionally. Simmer for 5 minutes, or until the sugar has dissolved. Add the lemon and orange juice and simmer again for 5 to 10 minutes, or until the liquid looks syrupy.

Strain into a measuring jug and leave to cool. Rinse out the sterile bottles and funnel with warm water and fill with the cordial, leaving a small gap of ¾ inch between the top of the liquid and the top of the bottle. Close the bottle tightly.

Making & keeping: Make any time of the year. Will last 3 to 6 months if kept in the refrigerator. Otherwise use straight away or pasteurize (see box, page 13).

Opposite: Instant Lemon Sherbet

Instant lemon sherbet

This is a simple, refreshing drink to make and enjoy any day of the year. Equally easy to make with oranges, grapefruit, or limes, serve it in tall glasses over ice, adding a splash of vodka for adult entertaining.

Makes 1 quart

Thinly peeled zest and juice of 4 lemons

3 oz (about 22) sugar cubes

1 quart boiling water

To serve

12 ice cubes

5 oz (1¼ cups) raspberries or blueberries (optional)

You will also need

Plastic wrap

Citrus squeezer

Large heatproof jug and a serving jug

Cut the zest of the lemons into thin strips; wrap half the prepared zest in plastic wrap and reserve. Put the remaining zest and the lemon juice in the large heatproof jug with the sugar cubes. Add a boiling water to the jug, stir, cover and leave to cool. Strain into a second jug for serving and refrigerate.

Serve in tall glasses with a few thin strips of the reserved lemon zest and some cubes of ice.

Making & keeping: Make any time of the year and use immediately.

Lemon barley water

Lemon Barley Water is an English classic: a vibrant and refreshing drink with an evocative pearly haze. It can be made in a number of ways, depending on how you like it.

Makes 2 quarts

7 oz (1 cup) pearl barley

Thinly pared rind of 2 lemons

Juice of 3 lemons

2 quarts water

½ to ¾ cup granulated sugar, to taste

You will also need

2 x 1 quart (32 fl oz) bottles with lids, washed in hot soapy water

Put the pearl barley in a medium-sized pan. Add the water and lemon zest and leave for 30 minutes. Bring to a boil and strain while still hot. If you like a more barley-flavored, glutinous drink, leave the liquid to cool before straining. Add the lemon juice and sugar to taste. Leave to cool, then use a funnel to pour into bottles. Seal.

Making & keeping: Make any time of year but particularly in summer. Serve chilled. Will keep in the refrigerator for a week or so.

Gooseberry & sweet cicely cordial

This summer drink is my favourite: delightfully fragrant, with floral and citrus notes. The exquisite gooseberry is only to be found (happily) in season, in farmers' markets, or on a bush near you, perhaps at the "bottom of an English garden," where once it was said babies were found. Its partner here, sweet cicely, is an old-fashioned plant with soft, downy, fern-shaped leaves, found in many herb gardens. Its leaves can be used to flavor drinks (see pages 182, 184) and vegetables and fruit such as rhubarb and gooseberry. The lightly aniseed flavor of the sweet cicely complements the gooseberry perfectly. Added to cocktails, ice cream sodas, and cakes, this is pure heaven!

Makes 1 pint

9 oz (about 2½ cups) ripe gooseberries

Thinly peeled zest of 1 lemon

1¼ cups granulated sugar

1 large bunch of sweet cicely, or a small bunch of rosemary or thyme

1 cup cold water

You will also need

Scissors

2 x 8 fl oz or 1 x 1 pint (16 fl oz) sterilized bottles, preferably glass, with screwcaps (see box, page 13)

Trim the top and bottom of the gooseberries with scissors. Rinse in cold running water, drain, and leave to dry on a clean cloth, or in the sun if the weather allows.

Put the washed fruit into a saucepan, add the lemon zest, half the sugar, the bunch of sweet cicely or other herbs, and half the water, then bring gently to a boil, stir to dissolve the sugar, and simmer for 10 minutes.

At the same time, put the remaining sugar in a small saucepan with the rest of the water and gently bring to a boil, stirring to dissolve the sugar. Simmer to reduce by one-third. Be careful not to reduce any more or else the syrup will caramelize.

Pour the syrup into the saucepan with the fruit and stir. Strain the mixture through a fine sieve and leave to drain over a bowl.

Cool, then pour into a measuring jug. Check the quantity and make up to 1 pint (16 fl oz) with boiling water if necessary.

When ready to bottle, rinse out the sterile bottles with warm water, fill with the spiced cordial using a funnel, leaving a small gap of ¾ inch between the top of the liquid and the top of the bottle. Screw down the cap firmly.

Making & keeping: Make in early summer. Will last 3 to 6 months if kept in the refrigerator. Otherwise use straight away or pasteurize (see box, page 13).

Note: If you don't have sweet cicely, try using a little star anise to re-create the flavor.

Serving cordials 

Homemade cordials vary in strength, and on the whole tend to be weaker than commercially made ones. It is therefore important to taste a little before serving or using in a recipe. Dilute with still or sparkling water, tonic, lemonade, milk, Lemon Sherbet (see page 22), or soda water and add plenty of ice. Dilute with hot water in winter for a warming drink. Transform into mocktails by adding ginger beer and other family fizzes (see page 44), cocktails by adding liqueurs (see page 116) and punches by adding wine, cider, perry, beer, or sparkling wine (see pages 82, 76, 80, 65).

Opposite: Classic Blackcurrant Cordial (left, see page 26) and Gooseberry & Sweet Cicely Cordial

Classic blackcurrant cordial

This is a simple classic recipe that can be adapted to make any soft-fruit cordial. I make cordials in small batches, using 9 oz of fruit that will yield 14 to 16 fl oz (1¾ to 2 cups) of cordial. If you, on the other hand, have masses of fruit that need preserving, then this is a simple and relatively quick way to do it. All you need to do is to increase quantities. But you will need large bowls and pans to deal with it—and lots of bottles.

Makes 14 fl oz or 1 3/4 cups

9 oz (about 2 cups) blackcurrants, or other soft fruits, washed, drained and dried

1 1/4 cups granulated sugar

1 1/4 cups cold water

Thinly peeled zest of 1 unwaxed lemon or a pinch of citric acid

You will also need

2 x 8 fl oz sterilized bottles, with screwcaps (see box, page 13)

Strip the blackcurrants from the stalks using a fork and put in a saucepan. Add the lemon zest or citric acid, half the sugar and half the water. Bring gently to a boil, stirring to dissolve the sugar. Simmer for 10 minutes.

At the same time, put the remaining sugar in a small saucepan with the rest of the water and gently bring to a boil, stirring to dissolve the sugar. Simmer to reduce by one-third. Be careful not to reduce any more, or else the syrup will caramelize.

Pour the syrup into the pan with the fruit and stir. Pour the mixture through a fine strainer and leave to drain over a bowl. Cool, then pour into a measuring jug. Check the level and make up to 1¾ cups with boiling water if necessary.

When cool, rinse out the sterile bottles with warm water, fill with the cordial using a funnel, leaving a small gap of ¾ inch between the top of the liquid and the top of the bottle. Screw down the cap firmly.

Making & keeping: Make in midsummer. Will last 3 to 6 months if kept in the refrigerator. Otherwise use straight away or pasteurize (see box, page 13).

Variation: You can use blackberries, raspberries, loganberries, mulberries, elderberries, blueberries, gooseberries, and strawberries, currants (black, white or red), or a mixture of fruits.

Illustrated on page 25

Redcurrant water

Makes 1 pint

9 oz (about 2 cups) redcurrants, rinsed, drained and dried

5 oz (about 1 1/4 cups) raspberries, rinsed and drained

1 1/4 cups granulated sugar

1 1/4 cups water

You will also need

Jelly bag , scalded (see box, page 21)

2 x 8 fl oz sterilized bottles, with screwcaps (see box, page 13)

This is a cordial by any other name, except that the fruit and syrup are dripped through a jelly bag instead of through a strainer. This results in a crystal-clear liquid: hence the name 'water.' Dilute to taste and serve as a hot or cold drink. Or pour over vanilla ice cream to serve as a super-speedy dessert.

Strip the redcurrants from the stalks using a fork and put into a large bowl, add the raspberries and half the sugar, cover with a clean cloth, and leave overnight (*see pic* 1).

In the morning you will find the bowl full of beautiful red juices. Stir the fruit and put the mixture into a saucepan with 1¼ cups of water.

Heat gently to dissolve any remaining sugar crystals. Bring to a boil and simmer for 10 minutes. Leave to cool a little, then strain though a jelly bag suspended over a bowl to catch the juices (*see pic* 2). Leave until the fruit stops dripping.

Put the remaining sugar in a small saucepan with ½ cup + 1 tbsp of water and bring to a boil. Simmer to reduce by a third. Be careful not to reduce any further as the syrup will caramelize.

Combine the fruit juice and the syrup and leave to cool. Transfer the liquid to a measuring jug to check quantity, topping up to 1¼ cups with boiling water if necessary. When ready to bottle, rinse out the sterile bottles with warm water, fill with the cordial using a funnel, leaving a small gap of ¾ inch between the top of the liquid and the top of the bottle. Screw the cap down firmly.

Making & keeping: Make in summer. Use immediately, keep in the refrigerator for 3 to 6 months, or pasteurize (see box, page 13).

Variation: Experiment with other fruits using this method. Try mixing blackcurrants, strawberries, and raspberries to make Summer Fruit Water.

Opposite: Rose Petal Cordial

Rose petal cordial

This is my take on a quintessential summer drink made with frothy, fragrant elderflowers gathered from early summer hedges, described below. You can experiment with any edible flowers from your garden or from the countryside to see what works. Make just a small quantity —say, one quart—while experimenting.

Makes 1 quart

12 roses; must be homegrown and unsprayed

Juice and finely grated zest of 1 lemon

3 1/4 cups cold water

1 lb 2 oz granulated sugar

Juice of 1 orange

1 tsp citric acid

You will also need

Muslin cloth, cheesecloth or jelly bag, scalded

4 x 8 fl oz or 2 x 1 pint (16 fl oz) sterilized bottles, with screwcaps (see box, page 13)

Strip the petals from the roses and place them with the finely grated lemon zest into a large, deep bowl. Pour in the cold water, cover with a clean cloth, weighing down the corners with clothespins to prevent the cloth from slipping into the liquid. Leave overnight.

The next day, suspend a cheesecloth or scalded jelly bag (see box, page 21; *pic* 2, page 27) over a large saucepan and pour the liquid and petals into the bag. When the liquid stops dripping, discard the contents of the bag.

Strain the orange juice, and add with the citric acid and sugar to the pan. Warm on low heat and cook gently to dissolve the sugar; stir and then simmer for a few more minutes. Pour through a strainer into a measuring jug.

Once cool, rinse out the sterile bottles with warm water and fill using a funnel, leaving a small gap of ¾ inch between the top of the liquid and the top of the bottle. Screw the lids down securely.

Making & keeping: Make all summer long. Will last 3 to 6 months if kept in the refrigerator. Otherwise use straight away or pasteurize (see box, page 13).

Elderflower cordial

Makes 1 quart

25 elderflower heads, shaken to remove any insects

1 1/2 quarts boiling water

2 lb 3 oz granulated or superfine sugar

Strained juice and thinly pared zest of 3 lemons and 1 orange

1 heaped tsp citric acid

You will also need

Cheesecloth or cotton jelly bag, scalded

4 x 8 fl oz or 2 x 1 pint (16 fl oz) sterilized bottles, with screwcaps (see box, page 13)

Strip the flowers from their stems, using the prongs of a fork to speed up the process. Put the flowers and the zest into a large deep bowl. Add a boiling water. Cover the bowl with a clean cloth, weighting the corners with clothes pegs to prevent the cloth from slipping in the liquid, and leave overnight.

The next day suspend a cheesecloth or jelly bag (see box, page 21; *pic* 2, page 27) over a large saucepan and pour the liquid and flowers into the bag. When the liquid stops dripping, discard the flowers and add the sugar, citric acid and strained citrus juice to the elderflower liquid. Heat gently to dissolve the sugar, stir, and simmer for a few more minutes. Strain into a measuring jug and leave to cool.

Once cool, rinse out the bottles with warm water, fill with the cordial using a funnel to ¾ inch below the top of the bottle. Screw the lids down securely.

Making & keeping: Will last 3 to 6 months if kept in the refrigerator. Otherwise use straight away or pasteurize (see box, page 13).

1

Monnica's marvelous medicine—raspberry vinegar

One summer's day, Monnica, one of my mature students, turned up to an Italian lesson with a small bottle bearing the words "Raspberry vinegar." She recommended it as a condiment, a refreshing summer drink, and a soothing potion for a sore throat. This was something new. I unscrewed the cap and breathed in the wonderful perfume of fresh raspberries. I poured a little into a glass, added water and was thrilled by the reviving sweet-and-sour flavor. Soon I was using it in salad dressing, drizzling a few drops onto steak and adding it to fruit salad. Start by making half the quantity to see if you like it as much as I do.

2

3

Makes 1 quart

14 oz (about 3 heaped cups) ripe raspberries

1³/₄ cups good-quality vinegar; cider vinegar is best

2 cups granulated sugar

4 x 8 fl oz bottles, washed in hot soapy water, with screwcaps (sterile bottles are not necessary where vinegar is concerned)

Carefully rinse the raspberries, drain, and leave to dry on a clean cloth (*see pic* 1). Once dry, put them into a large bowl, add the vinegar (*see pic* 2), and mash the fruit with the back of a wooden spoon to break it up (*see pic* 3). Cover with a cloth and leave for 3 or 4 days, mashing and stirring once a day. After this time, strain the mixture into a saucepan (*see pic* 4), add the sugar, heat, and simmer briefly to dissolve the sugar (*see pic* 5). Leave to cool.

When ready to bottle, rinse out the bottles with warm water, fill with the raspberry vinegar using a funnel, leaving a small gap of ¾ inch between the top of the vinegar and the top of the bottle (*see pic* 6). Screw the cap down firmly.

Making & keeping: Make in the summer. Will keep indefinitely at room temperature.

4

5

6

Artusi's siroppo* di frutta

Pellegrino Artusi is considered the father of Italian food as it is known in Italy today. He collected recipes wherever he went and compiled the famous Italian cookbook, *La Scienza in Cucina e l'Arte di Mangiare Bene*, gathering the best-known regional culinary traditions. In writing this book Artusi united Italy in a way that no one else has managed to do. Countless editions and many translations later, his birthplace, Forlimpopoli in Emilia-Romagna, is the home of a cultural institute and cookery school dedicated to his name. This *siroppo** is made with fruit and confectioners' sugar and no added water, and Artusi recommends it for its intensity of flavor. The fruit is left to ferment for several days before the juice is extracted, producing a syrup with a rounder, deeper flavor than other cordials.

Makes 7 to 14 fl oz

2 lb 3 oz raspberries, blackberries or blackcurrants

To every 8 fl oz (1 cup) of fruit juice produced add:

3 cups sifted confectioners' sugar

1/2 tsp citric acid

You will also need

Large, shallow terracotta dish

Fine strainer or light jelly bag, scalded (see box, page 21)

1 or 2 x 8 fl oz sterilized bottles, with screwcaps (see box, page 13)

** siroppo is the traditional spelling of sciroppo, as used by Pellegrino Artusi in his book La Scienza in Cucina e l'Arte di Mangiare Bene*

Put the fruit in a large, shallow terracotta dish, breaking it up with a potato masher. Cover with a clean cloth and leave to ferment—2 to 3 days for raspberries and blackberries, 4 to 5 days for blackcurrants.

Mash twice daily. If you forget to do this on the odd occasion you may see mold appearing on the fruit. If this does happen, simply push the mold back down into the fruit and mash well—it will be perfectly safe. Sugar acts as a preservative, and later on you will be boiling the resulting juice.

You will notice that the fruit "rises" overnight. This is the effect of the natural yeast contained in the fruit; what you are doing by mashing it is, to use a bread-making expression, "knocking it back." The idea is to keep doing this until the fruit stops rising. Blackcurrants tend to take longer than berries.

Put the fruit in a fine strainer or scalded light jelly bag set over a bowl and leave to drain naturally. Do not squeeze or press the fruit.

Measure the juice obtained so that you can calculate the amount of confectioners' sugar and citric acid required. Pour the juice into a saucepan and bring to a simmer. Add the confectioners' sugar and citric acid and stir until dissolved. Boil for 5 minutes.

Strain into a measuring jug and leave to cool. Once cool, rinse out a sterile bottle with warm water, use a funnel to fill with the *siroppo** up to ¾ inch below the top. Screw the lid down securely.

Making & keeping: Make in summer. Drink immediately, keep in the refrigerator for 3 to 6 months or pasteurize (see box, page 13). Diluted with still or sparkling water it makes a refreshing drink and its depth of flavors makes it perfect for making sorbet, granita or pouring over ice cream.

Syrop de menthe

Considering the fact that mint grows vigorously in every garden, we rarely make good use if it. Yes, we put it in mint sauce to go with lamb, use it to garnish Pimm's, and boil it with new potatoes, but seemingly its culinary uses stop there. Why not add it to salads and dressings and fruit desserts, and just before it starts to fade, make some of this delicious French syrup? It's perfect for making cooling summer drinks, and adding to fruit salads and sorbets.

Makes 1 pint

1¾ oz sprigs of mint—
a very large bunch

1 pint water

1 lb 2 oz (2 ⅔ cups)
granulated sugar

You will also need

1 x 1 pint (16 fl oz) bottle or a selection of small sterilized bottles to give as gifts, with screw- or swing-caps (see box, page 13)

Wash the mint and shake off the excess water, strip the leaves and discard the stems (*see pic* 1). Put the mint leaves in a bowl and add the boiling water and sugar (*see pic* 2). Stir well to dissolve the sugar. Cover with a cloth and leave for 48 hours, mixing and stirring occasionally.

Strain the liquid into a saucepan and discard the mint leaves. Put the pan over low heat, bring gently to a boil and stir to ensure that all the sugar has dissolved. Simmer for 5 minutes.

Transfer to a measuring jug. Rinse out the sterile bottles and funnel with warm water and fill with the syrup, leaving a small gap of ¾ inch between the top of the liquid and the top of the bottle. Seal.

Making & keeping: Make in summer and early autumn. Keep in the refrigerator for up to a year or pasteurize (see box, page 13).

Syrop de menthe extra

For a more refined and intense but less sweet-tasting syrup, try this recipe with no added water. Use it for flavoring candies, chocolates, and sparkling drinks.

Makes 8 fl oz

1¾ oz sprigs of mint—
a very large bunch—washed and shaken dry

12 oz (2 ½ cups) sifted
confectioners' sugar

Juice of 1 lemon

You will also need

Large mortar & pestle, or sturdy bowl and the end of a rolling pin

Cotton jelly bag, scalded
(see box, page 21)

1 x 8 fl oz sterilized bottle, with screw- or swing-cap
(see box, page 13)

Put the mint with the stems in a mortar with the sugar and lemon juice and work to a smooth paste with the pestle.

Cover with a clean cloth and leave overnight before straining through a scalded jelly bag suspended over a bowl (see box, page 21). Do not squeeze the bag or press the leaves.

When the dripping stops, put the syrup in a small saucepan and bring to a boil. Simmer for a few minutes, leave to cool and bottle as above.

Making & keeping: Keeps in the refrigerator for up to a year or pasteurize (see box, page 13).

Variation: To create a Far Eastern flavor, add a handful of jasmine flowers, bashed lemon grass, or a couple of knotted pandan leaves to the basic syrup ingredients instead of mint.

Spiced blackberry tonic

Blackberries are one of the delights of a waning summer. Garlands of plump, juicy, shiny, black fruit can be found out in the country and on roadsides for everyone to enjoy. If you know your territory, blackberries are the best reason for taking a walk at this time of year—but don't forget to take a plastic bag or maybe even a basket and a crooked-handled cane or walking stick. This is not for support but for beating back briars to move in close, or for hooking down those high blackberry stems that are dripping with fat fruit—and perhaps inevitably just out of reach.

Makes 14 fl oz

2 cups blackberries, washed, drained and dried

Thinly peeled zest of 1 lemon

2 1/4 cups granulated sugar

1 small pinch of ground cloves

1 good pinch of cinnamon

1 good pinch of ginger

1 cup cold water

You will also need

Cheesecloth or jelly bag, scalded

2 x 8 fl oz sterilized bottles, with screwcaps (see box, page 13)

Put the washed and dried fruit into a saucepan, add the lemon zest, half the sugar, the spices, and half the water (*see pic* 1). Gently bring to a boil, stirring to dissolve the sugar, and simmer for 10 minutes.

At the same time, put the remaining sugar in a small saucepan with the other half of the water and gently bring to a boil, stirring to dissolve the sugar.

Simmer to reduce by one-third. Be careful not to reduce it any further as the syrup will caramelize. Pour the syrup into the saucepan with the fruit and stir (*see pic* 2).

Strain the mixture through cheesecloth or a jelly bag and leave to drain over a bowl (*see pic* 3).

Allow to cool, then pour into a measuring jug. Check the quantity and top it up to 14 fl oz with boiling water if necessary.

When ready to bottle, rinse out the sterile bottles with warm water, fill with the spiced cordial using a funnel, leaving a small gap of ¾ inch between the top of the liquid, and the top of the bottle (*see pic* 4). Screw down the cap firmly.

Making & keeping: Make in late summer. Will last 3 to 6 months if kept in the refrigerator. Otherwise use straight away or pasteurize (see box, page 13).

1

2

3

4
KILNER
EST 1942

Previous pages: Spiced Blackberry Tonic (left, see page 36) and Carey Apple Juice

Carey apple juice

Carey Organic nestles in a rural valley at the end of a long and winding tree-lined lane, deep in England's Herefordshire countryside, not far from the River Wye. This recipe is based on owner Martin Soble's production methods, and includes his tip of including 20% cooking apples alongside the dessert apples for flavor.

Makes 1 gallon

26 lb 8 oz ripe dessert apples

6 lb 10 oz ripe cooking apples such as Bramley or Granny Smith

1 good pinch ascorbic acid

You will also need

Crusher and a basket or other form of apple press (see page 76). See also Note, right

Sterilized bucket (see box, page 13)

Wash all milling and pressing equipment in hot soapy water, rinse and leave to dry, or dry with a clean cloth

6 x 25.4 fl oz (75cl) sterilized green glass wine bottles with screwcaps (see box page 13)

Sort the apples, discarding any moldy ones and cutting away any bad or bruised parts. Position your crusher over the press. Feed the apples whole (skin and core), or cut in half if they are unusually large, into the crusher. The milled apple bits will fall into the press. When full, pack the apple down firmly (see page 76). Press out the juice and collect in a clean bucket. Add the ascorbic acid and stir.

Rinse out the sterilized bottles with hot water. Using a funnel, fill the bottles, leaving a small gap of ¾ inch between the top of the liquid and the top of the bottle. Screw down the caps.

Making & keeping: Make in late summer and autumn. Store in a refrigerator for a few days or pasteurize (see box, page 13).

Note: If you don't have a crusher, you can cut the apples into small pieces yourself, or you could invest in a Pulpmaster, but don't use a food processor because this will turn the apples to mush. I have found that if you want to make your own apple juice, you really need a decent basket press (see page 76). Otherwise, why not approach a cooperative or artisan juice producer and see if they will juice your apples for you?

Prohibition "cider"

During Prohibition in the early 20th century, the tradition of farm-made cider disappeared, to be replaced by apple juice production. Canny farmers continued to call the apple juice "cider." To this day many people in the United States still think of "cider" as a nonalcoholic drink. For this reason there is a distinction in the US between "cider" (pure apple juice) and "hard cider," which is the alcoholic drink the rest of us know and love. You will find recipes for the latter in the Beer, Cider & Perry chapter (see page 76). The recipe here is for pure apple juice.

Delicious fruit makes delicious juice

While selection of fruit is all-important, so is variety, ripeness, and condition. According to Martin Soble of Carey Organic, "If you are not prepared to eat your apples, then there is no point in making juice with them." The apples must be fully ripened for full flavor and good juice yield. Overripe fruit turns into a mush when pulped, and that can create problems with the juice once it is bottled. The crushing should result in small, clean pieces of fruit. While bruised, moldy, or damaged fruit should be avoided, small fungal spots on the surface of the apple skin do not affect the juice. Windfalls should be juiced as soon as possible before the bruising starts to ferment.

When we peel and cut apples for culinary purposes, we add lemon juice to prevent them from discoloring. In the same way, small amounts of ascorbic acid (vitamin C), 0.5% by volume (roughly a teaspoon per bucket), can be added to fresh juice to prevent it from darkening.

Once pressed, the juice should be bottled in green glass to prevent any further oxidation. To ensure that the juice doesn't ferment and turn to cider, the bottles should be carefully pasteurized (see box, page 13).

Vin cotto balsam

Well-known in Puglia, Italy, this age-old country syrup is made by cooking the first pressing of the *mosto* (crushed grapes for wine) for hours on end until it is reduced to a molasses-like syrup. Utterly delicious, it can be made at home by crushing grapes or figs and boiling the juice until it becomes syrupy. In Roman times *vin cotto balsam* was used in place of sugar. Today it is used to sweeten specialty cookies, ice cream, and drinks. Traditionally it is taken as a soothing tonic. When *vin cotto* is aged, it can be used like balsamic vinegar to anoint cheese, risotto, and game dishes. If you have your own vine, make this in bigger quantities. If not, try making it by reducing 2 quarts of pure grape juice to a molasses-like syrup.

Makes 1/2 to 1 cup

6 lb 10 oz very sweet grapes, red or white

You will also need

Jelly bag, scalded

1 x 8 fl oz or 2 x 4 fl oz sterilized bottles, with screwcaps (see box, page 13)

Put the grapes in a large, shallow bowl. Using a potato masher or your hands, crush the grapes as much as possible. Leave overnight to encourage the juice to flow, mashing again from time to time.

Squeeze the grapes in your hands to help extract as much juice and flesh as possible from the skins. Transfer the grape pulp to a scalded jelly bag (see box, page 21) suspended over a stainless-steel pan and leave until the bag stops dripping. If you are making large quantities, discard the bulk of the skins before putting the grape flesh and juice in the jelly bag.

When the grape juice has stopped dripping, discard the contents of the jelly bag and put the pan of juice on the lowest-possible heat. Cook, oh-so-slowly, for an hour or more, until the *vin cotto* is thick, sweet and syrupy. Once cool, use a funnel to fill your bottles, leaving a small gap of ¾ inch between the top of the liquid and the top of each bottle. Screw down the cap firmly and keep cool.

Making & keeping: Make in autumn, or when grapes are plentiful. Keeps indefinitely.

Variation: Use dried figs to create syrup of figs, or "figgy medicine" as it used to be known by those British children who took it as a cure-all or tonic. Cover the figs in cold water and leave to soften. Bring gently to a boil and cook until figs and water become a runny paste; proceed as above.

Rosehip syrup

Rosehip syrup was a staple in many great-grandmothers' medicine chests, fed by the spoonful to small children on a daily basis and taken by adults as a remedy for all kinds of ills. Today, like so many other natural remedies, the rosehip has been exalted to superfood status, and modern science is now proving what our grandmothers knew intuitively: that rosehips have potent anti-inflammatory properties. See also page 190.

Makes 1 pint

3/4 lb rosehips

1 3/4 cups granulated sugar

1 tsp citric acid

1 quart water

You will also need

Food mill or Mouli-legume

Jelly bag, scalded

1 x 1 pint (16 fl oz) bottle, or a selection of small, sterilized bottles to give as gifts with screw- or swing-caps (see box, page 13)

Roughly crush the rosehips in a food mill or Mouli, being careful not to reduce to a paste. Put in a saucepan and cover with 1 pint of boiling water, bring back to a boil and leave to stand for an hour or so, then strain into a bowl. Cover the juice with a clean cloth, put the crushed hips back in the pan and add another pint of water. Bring back to a boil and leave to cool. Leave overnight in the pan.

The next day, strain the liquid, discard the pulp, and put both juices in a pan. Add the sugar and citric acid, put on a low heat, and stir to dissolve before simmering for 5 minutes.

Pour the mixture through a scalded jelly bag and leave to drain over a large bowl (see box, page 21). Cool, then pour into a measuring jug, check the quantity and make up to 1 pint with boiling water if necessary.

When ready to bottle, rinse out the sterile bottles with warm water, fill with the cordial using the funnel, leaving a small gap of ¾ inch between the top of the liquid and the top of each bottle. Screw down the cap firmly.

Making & keeping: Make in late summer or early autumn. Will last 3 to 6 months if kept in the refrigerator. Otherwise use straight away or pasteurize (see box, page 13).

Right: Vin Cotto Balsam (left) and Rosehip Syrup

Family fizz

Alcohol-free sparkling drinks

Alcohol-free sparkling drinks

Alcohol-free carbonated drinks can be made using various techniques: capturing the wild yeasts found on certain flowers; adding baker's yeast; adding carbonated water to cordials; or by adding a combination of cream of tartar, citric acid, and confectioners' sugar.

Wild yeast creates a light, soft froth which, once captured, keeps in a bottle for a year without any deterioration in flavor. These summery drinks are based on Elderflower "Champagne," which is a British tradition. Always make sure that you only use garden flowers that have not been sprayed. You can use sterilizing fluid, following the manufacturer's instructions, to sanitize flowers you are unsure of.

Other carbonated drinks can be made utilizing fresh or granular baker's yeast. This creates a cloudy, what is generally known as an "old-fashioned", drink, such as lemonade and ginger beer. There are also more rustic potions made with nettles, dandelion leaves, etc., that once would have been used as tonics, remedies, or cure-alls—not simply as refreshing drinks. These tend to have flavors that you will either love or hate. Again, there is plenty of room to experiment, but make sure you don't add more yeast than is recommended (see box below), especially if adding baker's yeast to fruit or flower syrup that may still contain active natural yeasts. On the whole, these drinks keep well for a month or so, but the flavor is often at its best between two days and two weeks.

The simplest way to make carbonated drinks is to add carbonated water to an extra-strength cordial. Choose a brand of water that has robust bubbles to get the best results. These spritzes should be made and drunk on the same day, especially if mixed in a glass bottle.

Adding sparkle to drinks makes them even more refreshing and attractive than their still counterparts. In the past, Epsom salts were added to drinks to give them instant fizz, but you can achieve the same effect by adding a mixture of cream of tartar, confectioners' sugar, and citric acid. Alternatively, add a mixture of 1½ level tablespoons baking soda, 3 level teaspoons citric acid crystals, and 1 level tablespoon confectioners' sugar to 2 quarts of a drink to make it fizz. Add half a teaspoon of the dry mixture per glass to make any drink fizz.

Warning!

Making your own carbonated drinks with yeast can be an almost literal minefield. I made a huge bottle of blackberry-ade, went away for a few days, and when I came back the plastic bottle had exploded and its contents were everywhere. I would therefore suggest that when making carbonated drinks containing yeast you make sure to use a tough plastic bottle, not a thin biodegradable disposable one.

When utilizing the natural yeasts in flowers, always use plastic—never glass—and never use more flowers than are specified in the recipe because this increases the fizz factor. Bottling in plastic simply causes the bottle to contort; if it were glass, it would burst. A plastic bottle feels rigid to the touch as pressure builds. You should carefully release this build-up of pressure in the bottle by giving the cap a quarter turn to loosen it, then tightening it up again.

Once made, carbonated drinks must be conditioned in their plastic bottles for 48 hours, at which point they can be transferred to glass bottles or jugs for immediate use. If, however, they are not for immediate use, leave in the plastic bottles, following the quarter-turn rule every day as specified in the recipe.

Opposite: Fennel Flower "Prosecco"

Opposite: Fennel Flower "Prosecco"

Fennel flower "Prosecco"

If you have fennel growing wild in your garden, you'll be familiar with the dainty, soft, yellow flower heads that proliferate in late summer, attracting bees and other garden insects. The flowers have a delicate floral scent reminiscent of aniseed. If you love Sambuca and Pernod and the taste of food flavored with the more stridently flavored fennel seeds, you will enjoy this "Prosecco." Made using delicate, fragrant flowers, it is simple to produce and can be consumed within two weeks of being made. The bubbles create the delicate *spuma* (mousse) of a good Italian fizz. Experiment with the scented flowers of other herbs in your garden, too!

Makes 2 1/2 quarts

6 large fennel flower heads, well-shaken to remove any insects

Juice and finely grated zest of 1 lemon

1 1/2 cups granulated sugar

1 tbsp white wine vinegar

2 1/2 quarts cold water

You will also need

2 x 1 quart (32 fl oz) + 1 x 1 pint (16 fl oz) sterilized plastic (PET) bottles, with screwcaps (see box, page 13)

Pick the flower heads when in full bloom and put into a large bowl with the lemon juice and zest, sugar, and vinegar (*see pic* 1, opposite).

Add the water, stir, and let stand for 24 hours (*see pic* 2, opposite).

Put a piece of cheesecloth in a funnel and strain the liquid into the bottles. Seal and leave for 2 weeks, by which time your Fennel Flower "Prosecco" will be ready to drink.

Making & keeping: Make in mid- to late summer. Keeps for a year in a cool place. Once opened, drink within a few days before the sparkle subsides. See Warning box (page 46).

Illustrated also on page 47

Elderflower "Champagne"

This is simple and quick to make. It's light and refreshing, but hugely drinkable and it's ready within a couple of weeks after picking the flowers. It is said that you should only use flowers picked in the early morning and never pick them after rain, but I have picked in the afternoon and haven't had any problems. Certain varieties of elder produce flowers with a very unpleasant smell; whatever you do, don't use these.

Makes 1⅓ gallons

3 large elderflower heads, well-shaken to remove any insects

Juice and finely grated zest of 1 lemon

3 cups granulated sugar

2 tbsp white wine vinegar

1⅓ gallons cold water

You will also need

5 x 1 quart (32 fl oz) sterilized plastic (PET) bottles, with screwcaps (see box, page 13)

Pick the elderflower heads when in full bloom. Put into a very large bowl and add the lemon juice and zest, sugar, and vinegar. Add the water, stir, and let stand for 24 hours.

Put a piece of cheesecloth in a funnel and strain the liquid into the bottles. Seal and leave for 2 weeks, by which time your Elderflower "Champagne" will be ready to drink.

Making & keeping: Make in early summer. Keeps for a year in a cool place. Once opened, drink within a few days before the sparkle subsides. See Warning box (page 46).

Sparkling lemonade

This is a simple way to make a classic sparkling citrus drink. Make the fruit syrup in advance and add the sparkling water when required. As an alternative to sparkling water you could use tap water and, as was recommended by Fannie Farmer in her 1923 edition of *The Boston Cooking-School Cook Book*, add Epsom salts.

Makes 1 quart

1 cup cold water

2/3 to 1 cup granulated sugar

1 cup freshly squeezed lemon or other citrus fruit juice—roughly equivalent to 6 lemons, 7 limes, 4 oranges, or 3 grapefruit

1 1/3 pints sparkling water

You will also need

1 x 1 quart (32 fl oz) bottle washed in hot soapy water

Put the cold water in a medium-sized pan with ¾ cup of the granulated sugar, bring to a boil, then simmer for 3 minutes. Add the fruit juice and reheat briefly. Taste, and if necessary add the remaining sugar. Pour into a clean measuring jug and leave to cool.

When cold, pour the syrup into a bottle using a funnel and add the sparkling water. Close the bottle and chill. This lemonade is best made and consumed within 24 to 48 hours. As long as you are not going to keep this for more than a day or two, it will be fine in glass.

Making & keeping: Make when citrus fruit is at its best. Keeps for a few days in a cool place. Drink before the sparkle subsides. See Warning box (page 46).

Sparkling orangeade

Back in the fifties, orangeade, orange pop, or orange soda, as it was called, was a favorite choice in US soda fountains and drugstores throughout the world. Such drinks were so popular that they were even delivered to the door once a week. At the time orangeade was a lurid shade of orange; this recipe makes a rather more natural-looking orange drink.

Makes 2 quarts

Finely pared rind and juice of 5 oranges

Finely pared rind and juice of 1 lemon

8 to 10 1/2 oz sugar cubes, depending on preferred sweetness

1 tsp cream of tartar

2 quarts boiling water

2 tsp fresh baker's yeast, or 1 1/2 tsp active dry yeast

Pinch of superfine sugar

4 tsp warm (not hot) water

You will also need

Large earthenware crock or deep bowl

2 x 1 quart (32 fl oz) sterilized plastic bottles, with screwcaps (see box, page 13)

Put the oranges and lemon rind and juice in a large crock or deep bowl (the depth helps the yeast work properly). Add the sugar cubes and the cream of tartar. Pour the boiling water over the top, stir, and leave to cool until lukewarm.

When the liquid has cooled sufficiently, mix the yeast and superfine sugar with the warm water, stir into a paste, and add to the liquid. Cover with a clean cloth and leave for 48 hours.

Using a slotted spoon, skim and discard any debris that may have floated to the surface. Strain into a large jug, then use a funnel to pour into bottles.

Making & keeping: Make when citrus fruit is at its best. Keeps for 2 to 4 weeks in a cool place. Once open, drink within a few days before the sparkle subsides. See Warning box (page 46).

Variation: Using the same method, try other "-ades" to make lime or grapefruit fizz.

Opposite: Sparkling Lemonade (left) and Sparkling Orangeade

Nettle beer

Nettle beer is another nonalcoholic drink with an alcoholic-sounding name. In the past, it was made in quantity in the UK as a tonic and to refresh haymakers, back when working in the fields was thirsty work for lots of willing hands. Like many other artisan drinks, it has an acquired but pleasing taste with a nuance of beer. Unlike many such drinks, however, it is not sweet at all and is therefore very refreshing and thirst-quenching. Nettles have many healing qualities and have long been considered wonder plants, packed with vitamins, minerals, iron, and calcium. They are a remedy against many ills, such as rheumatism and arthritis, and are used in treating allergies, anemia, and kidney diseases.

Makes 1 to 1 1/3 gallons

1 lb 2 oz nettles

1 1/3 gallons cold water

1/2 cup turbinado sugar

1/2 tbsp fresh baker's yeast

You will also need

Colander or large strainer and cheesecloth

Baby-bottle sterilizing solution made according to the manufacturer's instructions

5 x 1 quart (32 fl oz) sterilized plastic (PET) bottles with screwcaps (see box, page 13)

Wear rubber gloves and gather a plastic bag full of mature nettles. Strip the leaves from the stems and immerse them in a large bowl filled with the sterilizing fluid. Leave to stand as directed.

Rinse and drain the nettle leaves thoroughly and put in a large pan with the cold water. Bring to a boil, then simmer briskly for 45 minutes.

Add the sugar and stir until dissolved (*see pic* 1). Strain into a large bowl through a colander or large strainer lined with a piece of cheesecloth. Let cool until lukewarm (*see pic* 2).

Crumble the yeast over the surface (*see pic* 3), then cover with a clean cloth. Leave the yeast to work (ferment) for 48 hours. Skim off any scum that may have formed using a slotted spoon and use a large jug and funnel to pour into bottles. Seal and store for a few days before drinking.

Making & keeping: Make all summer long and into late autumn. Keeps for 4 to 8 weeks in a cool place. Once open, drink within a few days before the sparkle subsides. See Warning box (page 46).

Lavender spritz

Lavender has such a lovely, lingering scent as you brush against it that it's very tempting to want to harness that fragrance to make cookies and cakes. If you love sweet, flowery flavors, try this lavender spritz. You can make the lavender syrup—the base for the drink—in advance and keep it in the refrigerator to make the spritz as and when you need it.

1

2

3

Makes 2 quarts

For the lavender syrup

2 oz lavender flowers

4 cups confectioners' sugar, sieved

Juice of 2 or 3 lemons

1/4 cup just-warm boiled water, if required

For the spritz

1 cup lavender syrup

2 quarts carbonated water with strong bubbles

You will also need

1 x 8 fl oz sterilized glass swing-cap bottle for the syrup*

2 x 1 quart (32 fl oz) sterilized glass swing-cap bottle for the spritz*

* See box, page 13

Put the lavender in a heavy-duty bowl and add the confectioners' sugar (*see pic* 1). Work to a smooth paste with the juice of 2 lemons (*see pic* 2), crushing the flowers with a spoon or the end of a rolling pin as you do so. Cover and leave overnight.

In the morning, stir the paste; if it has hardened a little, add the juice of a third lemon. Transfer the paste to a small pan and put on a low heat until the sugar has dissolved, stirring constantly (*see pic* 3); do not leave or cook for too long—otherwise, the paste will discolor. Transfer to a fine strainer and leave to drip over a bowl (*see pic* 4). When the liquid has stopped dripping, stir.

The syrup should be thick but have a pouring consistency (*see pic* 5). If the surface has crystalized a little it may be necessary to add ¼ cup of just-warm boiled water and stir well. Measure and bottle.

When you are ready to make the spritz, simply put ½ cup of the lavender syrup in a 1 quart swing-cap bottle, top up with carbonated water, and use within 24 hours (*see pic* 6).

Making & keeping: Make the syrup all summer long. Keeps for a year in the refrigerator. Once the water has been added, drink immediately. See Warning box (page 46).

Previous pages: Lavender Spritz

Ginger Beer

Homemade Ginger Beer is one of those English drinks that immediately conjures up days gone by, when harvest was a time for all the family to get into the fields and help out—not just the farmer and the farmhands. Consequently, there was generally a party atmosphere, and once the job was done, there would be cake, sandwiches, and Ginger Beer to wash the day's work away.

Makes 2 quarts to 3 quarts

½ a lemon

1 to 2 oz fresh ginger root, according to taste

2 quarts boiling water

9 oz sugar cubes

1½ tsp cream of tartar

2 tsp fresh baker's yeast

1 tsp superfine sugar

You will also need

Earthenware crock, very large deep bowl or large stainless-steel pan

3 x 1½ pints (24 fl oz) sterilized plastic (PET) bottles, with screwcaps (see box, page 13)

Pare the lemon zest thinly using a potato peeler, avoiding the white pith; squeeze the juice, strain, and reserve. Bruise the fresh ginger using a rolling pin or wooden mallet.

Pour the boiling water into a crock, very large deep bowl, or large stainless-steel pan. Add the bruised ginger, sugar cubes, cream of tartar, the lemon zest and juice, and leave to cool until lukewarm.

Mix the yeast and superfine sugar to make a paste. Add this to the other ingredients and stir well. Set the bowl over a tray to catch any spillage and leave to stand overnight.

In the morning skim off any debris that might have formed on the ginger beer using a slotted spoon; strain into a large jug and use a funnel to pour into bottles. Screw down the lids. The ginger beer is ready but improves if allowed to steep in the bottle for 2 days. Take care when opening the bottles; Ginger Beer is likely to be very lively! Transfer to a jug to serve if you don't want to pour from a plastic bottle.

Making & keeping: Make all year round. Keeps for a week or so in a cool place. Once open, drink within a few days before the sparkle subsides. See Warning box (page 46).

May's dandelion, ginger & licorice beer

When I visited Brian Fowler (see pages 85, 110), I discovered his wife May's recipe for Dandelion Beer in an album of family wine recipes she had compiled as a girl. It is an excellent thirst-quencher and tonic with amiable qualities. Recent research ranks dandelions in the top four green vegetables for overall nutritional value. The list of its curative properties is so remarkable that it's worth trying whatever the ill. Instead of cursing the dandelions in our gardens, we should celebrate them. Gather the leaves to make salads and hot or cold drinks.

Makes 1 1/3 gallons

1/2 oz licorice root

1/2 oz root ginger

1 oz fresh dandelion leaves

1 oz fresh hops or 1/2 oz dried hops

1 1/3 gallons water

1 lb 10 oz turbinado sugar

2 tsp fresh baker's yeast, or 1 1/2 tsp active dry yeast

You will also need

Small cheesecloth

Earthenware crock or very large bowl

5 x 1 quart (32 fl oz) sterilized plastic (PET) bottles, with screwcaps (see box, page 13)

Bruise the licorice and ginger root with a rolling pin or wooden mallet. Put the leaves, hops, licorice, and ginger in a small cheesecloth and attach to the handle of a large saucepan. Add the water. Bring to a boil, then simmer for 5 minutes. Strain into the crock or large bowl, add the sugar, and allow to cool until lukewarm. Add the yeast, mix well, and let stand for 12 hours. Use a large jug and funnel to pour into bottles and seal.

Making & keeping: Make spring and summer through to late autumn. Keeps for 4 to 8 weeks in a cool place. Once open, drink within a few days before the sparkle subsides. See Warning box (page 46).

Cranberry fizz

On festive occasions this stunningly colorful drink can be dressed up for the non-drinker at the party. Vary the ingredients to make vibrant fizz at any time of the year: rhubarb in spring, soft fruits and cherries in summer, and blackberries in the autumn.

Makes 2 quarts

1 lb 2 oz cranberries

Finely pared rind and juice of 1 lemon

Finely pared rind and juice of 1 orange

10 ½ oz sugar cubes

1 ½ tsp cream of tartar

2 quarts boiling water

2 tsp fresh baker's yeast, or 1 ½ tsp active dry yeast

Pinch of superfine sugar

1 fl oz warm (not hot) water

You will also need

Large earthenware crock or deep bowl

Food mill or Mouli-legume

2 x 1 quart (32 fl oz) sterilized plastic (PET) bottles, with screwcaps (see box, page 13)

Put the fruit in the crock or deep bowl and crush with a potato masher or the end of a rolling pin or—even better—put it through a food mill. Add the citrus zest and juice, sugar cubes, and cream of tartar. Pour the boiling water over the top, stir and leave to cool until lukewarm.

When the liquid has cooled sufficiently, mix the yeast and superfine sugar with the warm water, stir into a paste, and add to the liquid. Cover with a clean cloth and leave for 48 hours.

Using a slotted spoon, skim and discard any debris that may have floated to the surface. Strain into a large jug and use a funnel to pour into bottles.

Making & keeping: Make in winter. Keeps for 2 to 4 weeks in a cool place. Once open, drink within a few days before the sparkle subsides. See Warning box (page 46).

A global resurgence

Beer, cider & perry

Troubleshooting!

Sometimes the fermentation process doesn't always go to plan. If after a couple of days there is no froth on the surface of your wort (see Glossary*), no activity through the airlock (if using), or no characteristic fermentation odor it means that the yeast has failed to start the fermentation process. This can be for many reasons.

- Is everything adequately sealed or screwed down tightly enough? If the airlock grommet and/or fermenter lid are not fully sealed, the wort may be fermenting, but the CO_2 gas will be escaping through the faulty seal. Simply remove the fermenter lid and examine the wort for signs of fermentation: for example, condensation inside the lid, frothing/bubbling on the surface of the wort, and/or a ring of scum on the fermenter wall above the wort. Repair the faulty seal and ensure that the fermenter lid is screwed down properly.
- Was the wort too hot or too cold? The yeast needs particular conditions to start multiplying before it can begin converting sugars to alcohol and CO_2. If the wort was too cold, the yeast could still be dormant or not working fast enough. Move the fermenter to a warmer spot (64 to 73°F) and get the yeast going by stirring the wort with a sterilized spoon (see Glossary*). If the wort was too hot—above 95°F—this will kill or stun the yeast, resulting in slow or no fermentation. Move the fermenter somewhere cooler. When the wort has cooled to 64 to 73°F, stir in another sachet of yeast.
- Was the yeast past its sell-by date? Dried yeast only has a certain shelf life and can lose its potency with time or if exposed to air or moisture. Make sure the packet of yeast is within its sell-by date and not damaged. Keep yeast envelopes in a cool, dry place. If you suspect your yeast is too old, simply stir in a new packet to get the fermentation going.
- Did you forget to add the yeast? It happens! If you're unsure, add another one and start again.
- Has fermentation finished? Check the final gravity (see Glossary*) with your hydrometer to see, and if so, it's time for the next decision: bottle or pressure barrel.

* *Glossary can be found on page 196*

Beer

Craft beer, like cider and perry, is enjoying a universal resurgence. For years it was as if the fate of the brewing industry lay in the hands of huge international conglomerates, producing beers that were universally acceptable but lacked any great character. Slowly the voice of the discerning beer-drinker, both young and old, began to be heard, calling for beers with true taste, and miraculously the microbrewery movement was born. Microbreweries mushroomed in cities, towns, and out in the sticks on both sides of the Atlantic, and suddenly the big brewers began taking note. North American brewers traveled to Europe to see what was going on, and then discovered the cider revolution in the process (see page 70).

Beer is different to most of the other drinks in this book because, apart from so-called green-hop beers, made in the fall with freshly harvested hops, it isn't seasonal. Thus, beer can be made at any time of the year, using a specific recipe of malted barley, water, brewing salts, dried hops, and yeast. Most beers, unlike wines and liqueurs, can be drunk almost immediately, since aside from some aged beer styles, they don't improve with age.

One of the reasons that beer is made and enjoyed worldwide, over and above its obvious drinkability, is that it can be made from many staple carbohydrate sources, such as potatoes, rice, wheat, and corn as well as barley. Indeed, brewers often make use of this fact.

Beginning with beer No book on homemade drinks would be complete without beer, but here we only have room to scratch the surface. I have visited many microbreweries and talked to experienced homebrewers and professional brewers alike and they all say the same thing: "Use a good kit to start with." Therefore that is what we will do on these pages, following the principles I have picked up along the way.

There was a time when every household brewed its own beer, so you may think that it can't be that difficult to produce a decent brew. While that might be true for the talented artisan drinks producer, modern brewing techniques have made contemporary beers much more sophisticated—and their imbibers more discerning. I suspect many of the beers of yesteryear might not be so popular today.

Homebrew kits contain everything you're going to need in concentrate form, the key point being that the tricky initial stage of converting starches to fermentable sugars has been done. If all you want is a hassle-free alcoholic beverage that tastes good enough, then this is the route for you.

If, however, you are not content with leaving the final taste of your brew to a manufacturer, and you would like to get more involved, then you can try customizing your kit recipe. Experiment by adding fruit juices, spice infusions, or extracts and other flavorings to suit your own taste and creativity (see box, page 68).

These two simple paths to homemade beers may well satisfy your needs or they may just be a stepping-off point to making your very own brew from grains. In the latter case I would refer you to such classics as *Home Wine Making and Brewing* by BCA Turner and *The Penguin Book of Home Brewing and Wine-making* by WHT Tayleur, or Graham Wheeler's more recent *Brew Your Own British Real Ale*.

Wayne's world: your local font of brewing knowledge

Your friendly neighborhood brewing shop is the brewing equivalent of the amateur winemaking clubs or wine circles. You can be sure that you will find someone who is endlessly patient and an enthusiastic and experienced homebrewer, and with whom you can talk through your trials and tribulations. Someone who can set you back on a successful path when things go wrong.

Wayne Sosna is the homebrewing expert in my local hardware store, and he has proven invaluable to my research over the past couple of years. So, rather than going online, seek out your nearest brewing supplier. It may surprise you to know that there is one near you, probably trading predominantly as a hardware store, where you can buy everything you need—and get some friendly advice while you're at it.

Making real ale the Woodforde's way

By using a kit, making beer could not be easier. Being supplied with cans of malt extract takes a lot of the work out of the brewing process. Choose a good brand that offers a wide range of beer kits that emulate all the classic styles; then you can select the style that suits you and follow instructions. You can either buy these ingredients as part of a microbrewery kit, in which case the extra equipment you will need will be included—from the fermenting bucket to the long-handled spoon—or you can just buy the ingredients box, which is made up of a couple of cans, yeast envelopes, and instructions.

Woodforde's Nog

The Woodforde's homebrew kits are made for the brewery by Muntons, using exactly the same malt and hop recipes as the brewery. You can choose either to bottle, or put your new beer in a pressure barrel. With the latter, you can sample your new brew whenever you want to.

Makes 6 gallons

Beer kit, containing 2 cans of concentrated wort—hopped malt extract—plus a packet of yeast, very similar to that used by the brewery (see Glossary*)

Sugar, for priming purposes

3½ quarts boiling water

5 gallons cold water

You will also need

Sterilizing solution (see box, page 13)

6-gallon fermentation bucket and lid

Long-handled stirrer

Siphon (plastic tube)

Pressure barrel (see Glossary*) or 46 returnable-type, 1 pint (16 fl oz) glass bottles with swing-caps or crown caps (see box, page 73)

Before you start, sterilize all beer-making equipment (see box, page 13) and put the cans from the kit in hot water for 5 minutes.

Open the cans and pour the concentrated wort into the fermentation bucket. At this stage, some kits require the addition of sugar but this one does not.

Add 3½ quarts of boiling water, stirring well, taking care not to splash your hands. Top up the wort to 6 gallons with cold water and mix again to ensure all the contents are fully dissolved.

Sprinkle the yeast over the wort, stir, and cover with the lid. Leave for 6 to 10 days in a warm place, ideally 64 to 68°F. Test the final gravity using a hydrometer (see Glossary*). If it remains constant below 1014, fermentation has finished for this rich, off-dry beer (see box, page 70).

Skim off any yeast debris floating on the surface. Siphon the beer into bottles or a pressure barrel (see Glossary*).

To condition the beer and give it a bit of natural sparkle, add ½ tsp of sugar per bottle before closing, or up to a maximum of 3 oz for a pressure barrel. Keep it in a warm place for 2 days to kickstart the secondary fermentation. Store in cool conditions for 14 days, to allow it to clear before drinking.

Making & keeping: Make any time of year and drink when ready. The pressure barrel keeps a month or so once opened, but try it to make sure before drinking.

Note: To ensure that the wort is warm enough, and to protect it from potential draughts, I like either to wrap the fermenter in a blanket or put a large cardboard box around it.

** Glossary can be found on page 196*

Customize your brew 

Want to immerse yourself further in the subject? Then why not start using unhopped liquid malt extract kits, to which you add your own choice of hops?

Here are a few other ways you can tailor the recipes to your own taste.

- Adding part crystal malt extract gives color, huge flavor, and character to beer. Aim for 5 parts standard to 1 part crystal malt.
- Fruit beers are popular now and you might like to experiment. Try adding 5 oz of fruit to a 6-gallon brew of light ale. Rowanberries and elderflowers were a traditional addition, but you can use blackcurrants, sloes, cherries, elderberries, redcurrants, raspberries, or strawberries. The choice is yours, but juice the fruit before adding and make sure the juice is at a temperature of 72°F when you put it in the mix. The fruit will add color, sweetness, and flavor.
- For spiced beers, add either extracts or simply make your own spiced infusion (see recipe below).
- Add ½ cup of molasses to 6 gallons of mild ale or porter to give it color, flavor and a 2.3% boost in alcoholic strength. If you're a coffee addict, you can add coffee grounds to an imperial stout recipe (see Glossary*) to make it extra smooth and flavorful. To give it more color, add some liquid caramel, and if you want to give it a red color (for Valentine's Day, say) add ½ cup of beet juice to the wort.

Whatever you choose, adding extra ingredients to your brew should be done 24 hours after the yeast has been added. Wild yeast present in the additions might throw the initial fermentation into a frenzy. It is also important not to introduce anything too far into the fermentation process, since it may impart unwanted bacteria that could adversely affect the final beer.

Once these additions have been made, leave the beer to complete its fermentation, measure the gravity to confirm, rack into a pressure barrel or bottles, add sugar, seal the bottles, and leave to condition as instructed in the Woodforde's Nog recipe (see page 66).

** Glossary can be found on page 196*

Festive spiced ale

This festive ale is based on the German *Gruitbier* tradition, which adds herbs or spices instead of hops to a brew. You can use any blend of spices that appeal to you. Be aware that less is more; overspicing can be unpleasant. If this time your beer needs more spice, next time add more. Whatever you do, remember to write it down!

Makes 6 gallons

Unhopped beer kit (see page 66)

½ cup water

2 tsp juniper berries

Knob fresh root ginger

1 cinnamon stick

1 nutmeg, lightly crushed

You will also need

Sterilizing solution (see box, page 13)

Fermentation bucket, stirrer, siphon, pressure bucket or bottles, as per Woodforde's Nog recipe, page 66

In a small pan, bring the water and spices to a boil very slowly, then simmer for 30 minutes. Let it cool to 72°F. Strain.

Add the spiced solution to your light ale or beer of choice a day after fermentation has begun, and continue as described in the box above.

Making & keeping: Make in the autumn or winter and keep for up to a month or 2. Keeps best in the cool.

Note: Be patient—it will require some experimentation to find just the right level of spiciness to suit your taste. Take it easy to start with; too much is not as pleasing as you might think.

Cider & perry

During the past two decades, cider and perry (a cider made from a certain type of pear) have enjoyed a huge revival. While cider is part of the cultural heritage in much of Europe, everyone from small cider producers to big brewery owners has been keen to get in on the craft cider – "hard cider" in the United States – act. Cider and perry are two of the oldest drinks made in the UK. Records are vague prior to the Norman invasion, but French conquerors are credited with planting orchards and introducing production methods in the 11th century. When the Pilgrims set sail across the Atlantic, they took their apples, expertise, and equipment with them, and began making cider and perry on the Eastern Seaboard. In the 18th and 19th centuries, there was a vibrant perry and cider industry in both New York State and Massachusetts. US President John Adams apparently drank a pint of cider for breakfast.

Cider apples & perry pears Cider can be made from all types of apples, although cider varieties are arguably the most sought-after. While pear cider can be made with any pears, perry can be made only from perry pears.

In England, cider is famously made not only in the Three Counties (Gloucestershire, Herefordshire and Worcestershire), but in the southwest, Wales, and in the east of the UK, where dessert apples dominate. Cider is made throughout the world, most notably in Brittany and Normandy in France, regions of Germany and northern Spain, the United States and Canada, Argentina, and more recently, Australia and New Zealand (see page 74).

A traditional process One autumn afternoon, I find myself with Martin Soble of Carey Organic at his Herefordshire farm. I watch as apples are loaded onto a conveyor and fed into the "grater," where they are cut up and then fall down onto a cloth-lined rack. The cloth has been laid out over a square wooden frame on top of a slatted base. Two men pack the grated apple into the cloth and then fold the four edges of the cloth across the apple pulp to form what is known as a "cheese." The rack is removed, a fresh base placed on top of the cheese, the rack is replaced, and the exercise is repeated up to a dozen times. Now high, the stack is carefully railroaded over to a 1930s hydraulic press, where 120 tons of pressure is applied and apple juice gushes out like water from a spring (see Carey Apple Juice, page 40).

This is the traditional way of extracting juice from apples for cider and juice alike. Many craft-cider and juice makers have gone over to continuous-belt presses, but Martin prefers this vintage system. He says it squeezes out every last bit of juice and flavor.

Alcohol & sugar

The alcohol by volume (abv) level of fermented drinks such as cider and perry varies according to the level of sugar in the fruit, which is itself dictated by the amount of sunshine it absorbs. Perry, for example, tends to vary between 5 and 7% abv. The abv affects the flavor of the cider or perry, and it is therefore difficult to achieve a constant recipe if the drink is to be a reflection of the taste of the fruit and the year it has experienced.

Beer is different in numerous ways, one being that you brew to a recipe, thus nailing the alcoholic quantity time and time again to your chosen abv percentage.

Sugar levels are important to keep yeast alive and running. The natural sugar content in the fruit allows the yeast to multiply so that it can then convert sugar to alcohol. While fermented natural sugar yields a better taste than added sugar, as with wine, if sugar levels are low, more can be added prior to fermentation to bolster the alcohol content. An added bonus of a higher-abv cider is that it keeps better. With beer, unlike with wines and ciders, not all the sugars in malted barley can be fermented into alcohol. Thus, while the final gravity reading measured with a hydrometer for fruit- and vegetable-based fermented drinks might approach 1000, beer can easily end up above 1010, when it will taste sweeter (see Glossary, page 196).

Craft

Both craft cider and perry are still, not sparkling (for sparkling perry, see page 80). These styles of cider and perry are undervalued, if not unknown, to most people, and the majority of UK pubs sell oversweet, tasteless drinks masquerading as the real thing, made with hardly a hint of apple or pear. What better reason for making your own?

Tom Oliver's rough guide

Tom Oliver is a world-renowned artisan maker of the very finest perries and ciders in a beautiful corner of England's rural Herefordshire, at the heart of the county's Cider Route. His craft is a lifelong passion that happens to make up only a chunk of his richly diverse life. He adheres strictly to the old traditions of these country crafts and is constantly trying to balance ethics and profits—not an easy thing to do in a competitive world. Tom still makes cider and perry the way it has been made for centuries: with 100% cider apples or perry pears and nothing else—no added water, no yeast other than what occurs naturally, no added sugar, and even no sulphites (usually added as a preservative).

If you have a perry-pear tree or a cider-apple tree near you, you may be tempted to try making your own. A few gallons made from scratch in your kitchen are, Tom says, "perfectly drinkable." "However, there is a correlation between taste, character, and volume." My usual advice to anyone new to a craft is to make a small amount to see how it goes, but Tom warns, "Some of the most challenging perry and cider I have ever made was in demijohns. As soon as you put it in a 200-litre [53-gallon] barrel, the benefits of volume are fantastic."

If you have access to a large tree, you should have plenty of fruit, and therefore a 53-gallon barrel may not seem daunting. That said, we have to start somewhere, and I source my cider apples from a nearby orchard. So let's start with a demijohn and see how it goes. And if we get good results in a demijohn, just think what we can achieve in a barrel.

Perry pears Perry trees such as Blakeney Red and Moorcroft are tall and stately. Some are two- or three-hundred years old, with branches that arch skyward, inviting the sun into their very core. In spring they wear a thick mantle of virgin-white blossom which, once spent, falls in drifts like snow.

Today, perry is primarily to be found in Gloucestershire, Herefordshire, and Worcestershire in England, otherwise known as the Three Counties. Perry is so rooted in this region that the Slow Food Foundation has recognized it as one of its international Presidia, set up to champion endangered food-and-drink heritage. The Three Counties Perry Presidium sets out designated areas and rules governing production.

The perry tree bears fruit in late summer, which is left on the trees to ripen until it falls. Some varieties fall over a matter of days, others over a period of weeks. Blakeney Reds, for example, start to fall in late September. The fruit is collected weekly until the third week in October, when pressing starts. This early fruit will make the first batch of perry of the year, just in time for Christmas. In Henry VIII's day, perry was recognized as much for its purgative as its alcoholic effects—hence its arrival was much anticipated.

Early crops have to be gathered and pressed within 24 hours, otherwise they spoil. Other varieties ripen during October and November—the later the harvest, the colder the weather and there is no rush to press the fruit; it can wait for a week or so if necessary.

Equipment

To start out you may want to have a dalliance with the craft to see how it goes—in which case it's possible to improvise with a food processor, a bucket, a large muslin bag, and a couple of demijohns. If, however, your intentions are honorable, you are going to need some equipment to help the process along.

- Sterilizing solution (see box, page 13)
- Plastic bucket to collect juice
- Basket press and mill—see pages 40, 76
- Demijohns—size and quantity will depend on how much you want to make
- 53-gallon (200-litre) barrel—if you're going to get serious about cider-making
- Yeast nutrient and yeast packets—optional
- Airlocks and stoppers to suit
- Hydrometer—to measure sugar content
- Siphon—plastic tube, for racking and bottling
- Plastic bottles or containers to suit, with screwcaps, *and/or*
- Crown caps and a crown capper

Cider & perry: a bigger picture

The amateur cider maker might well take inspiration from both Old and New World producers. While cider has been made in northern France for centuries, the process was originally introduced to North America by early settlers, where today it is a fast-growing industry.

Normandy cider Two thousand farms are still producing craft *cidre* (cider) from 100% fruit in the Pays d'Auge in the south of Normandy. A delightful 40-mile cider route takes you through Normandy countryside littered with welcoming idyllic black-and-white, tumbledown farms producing *cidre*, vinegar, Calvados (apple brandy), and *Pommeau* aperitif (a blend of Calvados and apple juice). Normandy cider and *poiré*, like British West Country cider and perry, is made predominantly with cider apples and perry pears.

Normandy cider is graded *doux, demi-sec, brut,* and *traditionnel*, translating as slightly sweet, medium-dry, dry, and strong. Strengths range from under 3% to over 4%, compared to British cider, which varies from 4 to 8%, depending on the season and the varieties being used.

Normandy *cidre bouché* is a naturally sweet, sparkling cider made by a traditional process called "keeving" that has all but disappeared in the UK. The apples are harvested and stored for several weeks in an apple loft to ensure maximum ripeness. Then, late in the year when the weather turns, the fruit is washed, carefully sorted, and milled. The pulp is then packed into barrels and left to stand for 24 hours.

Oxidation takes place, producing some color in the juice, but more importantly pectin leaches out of the apple cell walls into the juice. This maceration, or *cuvage* as it is called in France, has no equivalent in today's British cider-making, although it was apparently common practice in the mid-1600s. It produces juice that is richer in color and thicker in texture than juice that is pressed immediately.

The juice is run into clean vats, previously sulphited, and left to ferment with wild yeasts. Temperatures are low and fermentation is therefore slow to take off. The natural pectin esterase enzymes in the apple juice slowly change the pectin into pectic acid. This forms a gel as it cross-links with the natural calcium in the juice, and the gel rises to the surface to form a brown cap while some falls as sediment to the bottom, taking with it much of the protein and leaving clear juice in between. This is siphoned off into a second, clean, sulphited fermentation vat.

The fermentation is very slow because most of the nutrients in the juice have been discarded with the cap and the sediment. The result is a naturally sweet cider when racked into bottles, which can then be refermented in the bottle to create a natural fizz.

Pairing *cidre* with food

Although it is traditional to drink Normandy cider with food such as pancakes, other fruity desserts, or fish and poultry, it has a good apple fragrance and makes a refreshing drink by itself. Brut cider, with its darker golden color, delicate bubbles and the taste of mature, ripe fruit, is excellent drunk with red-meat dishes and cheeses such as Camembert.

Cider house rules USA Artisan cider-making in the United States is a huge topic. In the past, most people made their own alcoholic beverages. They did not sell it and they did not buy it; they simply made it for their own consumption. As commercial brewing took over in the early 20th century, people found they could go out and buy their liquor cheaply, and consequently cider went into decline.

Greg Hall of Virtue Cider is a Michigan craft cider-maker determined to turn this around. He believes he can turn southwest Michigan's fruit belt, where there are over 1,000 fruit growers, into the Napa Valley of the craft-cider industry. Greg was a master brewer with Goose Island on a fact-finding mission to the UK and France when he saw the potential of craft cider back home. His methods are classically European, influenced by his visits to Normandy and southwest England. Where the process differs is that the juice is initially pumped into stainless-steel tanks and left to settle before artificial yeasts are added. Once fermentation is complete, the new cider is transferred to barrels to age.

Following the British tradition, Greg believes how the fruit looks is not important. He is looking for different characteristics in the fruit: how it smells; how it tastes; the high acidity of fruit is essential. Aided and abetted by Herefordshire cider expert Tom Oliver (see page 73), he is experimenting with traditional methods. As a result, some juice goes into barrels at pressing and is left to ferment spontaneously.

A stateside survey

Today the Northeast produces more cider and perry than any other area of the United States, often using heritage (heirloom) apples. Arguably, however, the industry is more vibrant and innovative in the Pacific Northwest, where they are introducing French and British cider-apple and perry-pear varieties and also innovating with different techniques and types of products. In Oregon and Washington, for example, they are experimenting with chili-, fruit-, and hop-flavored ciders.

1

2

Three Counties cider & perry

Here we focus on the traditional still versions of cider and perry. I used late-ripening fruit collected in November, including Gin pears and a Jersey-type cider apple, possibly Harry Masters Jersey. Pick the fruit from the ground as soon as it falls and use it all. Ripe fruit imparts maximum flavor and yields more juice. If the fruit is an early-ripening variety, the fruit probably needs to be milled within 24 hours (see page 73). Traditionally the fruit was crushed in a tub with a big stick, but if you are making small quantities you could try using a food processor to chop the fruit, although this isn't going to be easy (see note, page 40). The juicing is hard to do without a basket press of some sort. If you want to start making fruit juices, cider, and perry on a regular basis, it's worth investing in a press and mill (see page 197), or tracking down a community juice- or cider-maker who can help you.

Makes 1 x 1 gallon demijohn/carboy

33 lb ripe cider apples or perry pears—blemishes, bruising, scabs, and all, but no mold

You will also need

Press and mill, plastic bucket, demijohns/carboys, airlocks and bungs, siphon, as per box, page 73

Glass or plastic bottles, to suit

Sterilize all your equipment (see box, page 13). Wash or rinse and dry the fruit in the air. Cut into pieces if the fruit is too big to feed into the mill or grinder (*see pic* 1). Transfer the milled fruit to the press. Set a clean bucket under the press to collect the juice. When the basket is full, press the fruit (*see pic* 2).

Transfer the fruit juice to a sterile demijohn, inserting a bung with an airlock on top (*see pic* 3). Store the liquid in a warm place to help the natural yeasts take hold (see box, page 78).

Wild yeast

The quantity of wild yeast in a sterile environment—that is, indoors in a clean demijohn/carboy—is much lower than outdoors in a barrel, so often apple and pear juices need warmth to start the fermentation process. As the yeast works on the sugars, alcohol and CO_2 are given off. The alcohol remains in the fluid and the CO_2 escapes through the airlock. The naturally occurring wild yeast sets to work early on, getting the alcohol level up to 1%, then others in the juice take over. If fermentation doesn't start, or gets "stuck" before all the sugars have been used up, consider adding some yeast nutrient (see Glossary, page 196).

Fermentation in this sort of environment can take about 2 months. When the bubbles stop or slow down, rack off into a second, sterile demijohn/carboy, take out the airlock, and put in a fresh bung and airlock (*see pic* 4). This will allow any remaining gases to escape.

Do not bottle your cider until the day you want to drink it (*see pic* 5), because, if any fermentation is still taking place, the bottles may explode. Alternatively, transfer to plastic bottles or containers.

Making & keeping: Make in the autumn. Early-ripening varieties will be ready by Christmas. Drink immediately, but it does improve with keeping—indeed, it will keep as long as you can resist drinking it.

Note: For those not investing in a fruit press, transfer the milled fruit to a large muslin cloth, tie it up, and suspend it over a large, non-corrosive receptacle to extract the clear juice.

5

Old English "Champagne": sparkling perry

Fine perry is "Champagne" made with pears! Okay, maybe that's a slight exaggeration, but through the ages, during the years that England was at war with France, Champagne and French wines disappeared from tables and English perry and ciders enjoyed a renaissance. Owners of great estates proudly served their own estate-made and -bottled vintages. While Three Counties Sparkling Perry is almost unheard of outside its homeland, I hope one day the pubs and restaurants in its terroir will become sufficiently proud of their fine native drink to keep a bottle chilled on the counter to sell by the glass, much as is done in the Veneto with Prosecco.

Makes 9 x 1 pint bottles or 6 x 75 cl Champagne bottles

1 x 1 gallon demijohn/carboy of freshly made perry (see page 76)

2/3 cup granulated sugar

1 packet of Champagne yeast

You will also need

Siphon

9 x 1 pint (16 fl oz) (or 6 x 1 1/2 pint/24 fl oz) sterilized dark-green plastic (PET) bottles with screwcaps or 6 x 75 cl Champagne bottles; checked for scratches, chips, or other damage

6 to 9 x polyethylene Champagne corks

6 to 9 x Champagne wires

2 x 6-bottle cardboard wine box

Ferment the perry and rack into a sterile demijohn/carboy. Do not add Campden tablets or other chemical yeast-inhibitor; otherwise, the secondary fermentation will not work.

Make the Champagne yeast starter as per the Modern Wine Model, step 4, (page 106). Dissolve the sugar in a small pan with ⅓ cup of the perry and gently heat to ensure all the sugar dissolves. Leave to cool.

Siphon the perry into the bottles up to a level 2½ to 3 in from the top of the bottle. Add ⅙ of the perry solution and shake the bottle well to mix the liquids. Add ½ tsp Champagne yeast starter and shake the bottle.

Ensure the level of the wine is 1 inch from the top of the bottle, top up with perry, or pour off as necessary. Fit a hollow white polyethylene Champagne stopper; it will need forcing in, then wiring down. Pack the bottles into the cardboard carton to minimize the effects of a possible burst.

Store inside for a week to help start the secondary fermentation and then transfer to a cool place for 6 months to a year. Each week turn the bottles with a short, sharp twist to prevent the yeast formed during this secondary fermentation from sticking to the side of the bottle. Do not shake.

Do this for 6 months, or until the perry is perfectly clear. Any yeast in the bottles should settle around the "punt"—the indentation in the bottom of the bottle.

Making & keeping: Make in late winter or early spring, depending on when your perry pears are harvested. Drink after 6 months if you must, but it will improve if kept for a year.

A very good year

The wine list

The wine list

In the good old days, it was common for people to make tonics and potions at home with the fruit, vegetables, flowers and berries that flourished nearby. Often referred to as wines, they were quite unlike the wines we are familiar with today. Tastes and customs change and the whole ethos of homemade wine making waned. Better times brought mass production and convenience food and eventually cheap booze.

Wines made at home, were not simply enjoyed as drinks but were lauded for their medicinal qualities and taken as tonics. With the arrival of modern medicines such beliefs were branded as old wives' tales. To my mind it is these old-fashioned remedies, the sweeter wines, the ones which retain the taste of the ingredients they are made with, that are the most enjoyable and successful.

Wines from nature You can make wine with any kind of fruit. In the past, many flowers were used, too: cowslips, primroses, pansies, elderflowers, clover, lavender, gorse and broom flowers, roses, marigolds, and dandelion petals. Root vegetables such as parsnips, celery, potatoes, and carrots all make good wine, as do wild berries such as rowan, blackberries, elderberries, rosehips, and many others growing near you. Herbs such as parsley, sage, rosemary, and thyme, and even weeds or wild plants such as nettles and cow parsley, also used to be popular.

Yeast

The type of yeast you use is up to you. For wines made with the Country Wine Code (page 86), I used naturally occurring wild yeast, or the trick of spreading fresh baker's yeast on toast and floating it on the must (*see pic* 5, page 101). For A Modicum of Modern Science (see page 102), after experimenting, I moved onto Super Wine Yeast Compound, a specially formulated wine-yeast mix that guarantees good results every time. If you prefer to keep it natural, use little packets of yeast specially designed for specific wine types (red, white, Champagne, etc). If the fermentation doesn't start or seems to stall part of the way through, see the Troubleshooting! box (page 64) to find out what the problem might be. If it doesn't work the first time, try, try, and try again. After all, home winemaking is trial, error, and finally, experience.

Unlike any other form of preserving, wine can be made with blemished fruit as long as it is ripe and contains plenty of sugar. It is therefore the answer to that excess of fruit you don't know what to do with; you don't even have to pick it from the tree or bush. You can simply let it fall, shovel it up from the ground, and put it in a big tub: blemishes, skin, and all.

I would not have the heart to strip a bank of its primroses nor an orchard of its cowslips since wildflower meadows are an uncommon sight these days and look so beautiful. While I can't ever imagine growing enough pansies or marigolds to make wine, dandelions grow profusely, and I soon found enough dandelion heads in our garden one sunny afternoon to make my first batch.

Starting out There are three ways of making wine: the old-fashioned way, which I refer to as the Country Wine Code (see page 86), the Modern Wine Model (see page 106), and the method that borrows a little from both, A Modicum of Modern Science (see page 102). This said, with a bit of care and translation, you can use any of the methods to make any of the recipes.

Country wines are made with seasonal ingredients, water, fruit, and yeast, and retain the integrity of the ingredients. These drinks reflect not only the flavor of the fruit and flowers, but also the season, the weather, the spot where the ingredients were gathered and the care and attention of the winemaker.

The Modern Wine Model sets out to make clear, stable wines that are vinous and do not necessarily reflect the taste of the fruit they are made with. The wine is made with all the benefits that both science and the contemporary wine industry can offer. However, even seasoned amateur winemakers say that wines made in this way can be hit-and-miss. Not every year is a good one!

This said, I do not rule out the possibility of aiding the country methods with a little modern science. Techniques such as boiling raw materials to destroy the enzymes responsible for oxidation and to create an essence, for example, and adding citrus fruit to add pectin to the mix to help fermentation and act as an antiseptic, can help. Some wines can be made without boiling the fruit, but simply mashing it and relying on the naturally occurring yeasts.

Finally, wines can be fortified with a measure of brandy, rum, gin, or spices before bottling to add extra flavor, strength, and keeping power (see page 114). After all, if you can enhance—or even save—a demijohn/carboy of wine by adding a little brandy, why not? And, as in previous centuries, chopped raisins can be added to wines for extra fortification and sweetness.

It is more complicated to make sweet wines. While fortified wines will retain sweetness because the added spirit stops fermentation before all the sugar is converted to alcohol, for unfortified wines the simplest way is to add a few teaspoons (to taste) of sugar syrup (see page 108) to a bottle of wine just before serving.

Join the club Amateur winemaking clubs are an important element for the beginner, and there are buoyant and convivial groups all over the place. They allow winemakers to compare notes, to taste each other's wines, and to improve their own methods.

An experienced voice When I started researching *Artisan Drinks*, I approached Gloucestershire's Newent Wine Circle to ask for expert advice. I was directed to Jean and Jim Haines and to champion amateur winemaker Brian Fowler. Jim and Jean have been making wine since the seventies and have made everything from rose petal to pea pod wine, with all the fruit wines in between. They started the Country Wine way, but today use modern methods and helped me devise my Modern Wine Model (see page 106).

Brian is now the president of the wine club he helped to found back in the early seventies. I met him in his garden one lovely summer afternoon when he treated me to his stories, his expertise, and shared his family recipes (see page 110). We later retired to his shed stacked with carefully labelled demijohns of fruit wines going back years. We sampled a few and he sent me home with a few more.

Before I left, we ambled around his orchard in the early evening sunshine, tasting plums and apples from the knarled old trees and discussing which varieties make the best wine. His advice is, "Do the right thing at the right time and you will be halfway there. Don't think 'I will do it tomorrow.' Just do it!"

Top tips

With his decades of experience, country winemaker Brian Fowler suggests the following:

- Freeze fruit before making wine—it breaks down the cell walls, thus aiding the winemaking process.
- Dark plums don't make good wine but yellow plums do.
- Old damson varieties that are tiny and pointed make good wine; modern varieties that are bigger and rounder do not.
- There is no need to remove stones from plums, or damsons.
- Small heritage varieties of gooseberries such as Careless make good wine.
- Heritage apple varieties found in old orchards and gardens make good wine.

For better wines, try the following blends and natural additions:

- Blends of fruit often work better than single varieties; for example, a mix of elderberries, sloes, blackberries, and blackcurrants make a rich red wine.
- Blend Spartan apples with grapes and heritage apples with grape juice before fermentation.
- Add 1 quart of grape juice to 2 quarts of core fruit juices—red for red berries and white for apples.
- For extra sweetness, follow the traditional route and add white raisins to white must, and raisins to red must at the start.
- To give tannins, add a cup of cold tea per 4 pints of wine.

How much?

While you are at the experimental stage, you may feel that a one-gallon demijohn/carboy of wine is too much. I have a couple of "demi"-demijohn that hold just four pints, allowing me to make smaller quantities. This is particularly useful when making flower wines, which require lots and lots of petal-picking.

The traditional route

These are the wines made as they have been for centuries, with nothing more than raw ingredients, sugar and time, although some use the old trick of using baker's yeast spread on toast. This method can be used to make wines in other sections too, just as the recipes in this section can be made with a little help from modern methods (see pages 102 to 112).

The country wine code

Follow the instructions for each individual recipe. Then:

1. Prepare the sweetened liquid ("must") as per your recipe. Pour into a glass demijohn/carboy, up to the shoulder where the vessel starts to narrow. Reserve any surplus to top up the level as necessary (see Still Wines route, below).
2. Put the demijohn/carboy on a tray; position it in a warm place. In a short time fermentation will start and froth will pour over the top of the vessel into the tray. Top up levels with the surplus wine. Should the liquid not start to ferment after a few days, try adding yeast (see step 4, page 106).
3. When the fermentation calms down and the froth no longer forms, clean up the tray, cover the demijohn/carboy with a folded cloth (*see pic* 6, page 91), and leave until fermentation is complete and bubbles stop forming.
4. Choose whether you would like a still or sparkling wine and follow the relevant steps below.

For still wines

- Put the demijohn/carboy in a cool room for 14 days.
- Use a rubber tube to siphon, or "rack off," the partially clarified liquid into a clean demijohn/carboy (see Glossary*), taking care to leave behind the yeast deposits.
- If the second demijohn isn't completely full, top up with spare must if you have it; otherwise use cooled boiled water. Insert a cork or seal firmly. Store in a cold cellar for 6 to 12 months.
- Remove the cork and rack off the clear liquid into bottles. Cork or cap firmly. Store the bottles on their sides for 6 months or longer.
- The longer the wine is stored, the better it will taste.

For sparkling wines

- Store the fermented wine as cold as possible for 14 days.
- Siphon the wine into another demijohn/carboy, taking care not to disturb the yeast deposits.
- Prepare sugar syrup by dissolving 1 cup of granulated sugar in 1 cup (8 fl oz) of boiling water for every gallon of wine. Leave to cool.
- Add the cooled sugar syrup to the wine, mix well, siphon into suitably strengthened bottles (see Glossary*), and cork and wire or tie down.
- Store bottles on their sides in a cellar or in the dark for 6 months.

These methods are for dry wines. For something sweeter, add more sugar syrup before serving.

* *Glossary can be found on page 196*

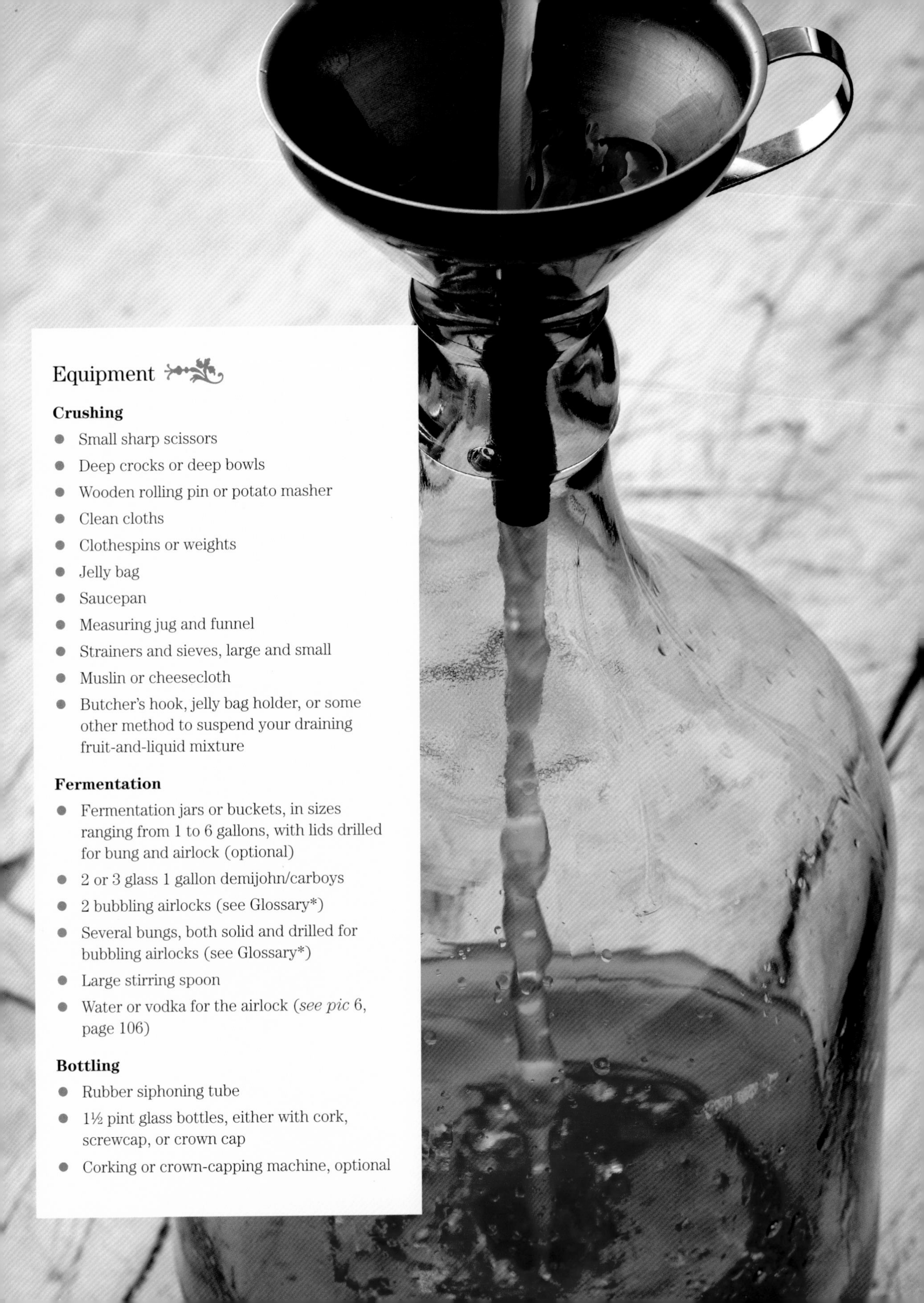

Equipment

Crushing

- Small sharp scissors
- Deep crocks or deep bowls
- Wooden rolling pin or potato masher
- Clean cloths
- Clothespins or weights
- Jelly bag
- Saucepan
- Measuring jug and funnel
- Strainers and sieves, large and small
- Muslin or cheesecloth
- Butcher's hook, jelly bag holder, or some other method to suspend your draining fruit-and-liquid mixture

Fermentation

- Fermentation jars or buckets, in sizes ranging from 1 to 6 gallons, with lids drilled for bung and airlock (optional)
- 2 or 3 glass 1 gallon demijohn/carboys
- 2 bubbling airlocks (see Glossary*)
- Several bungs, both solid and drilled for bubbling airlocks (see Glossary*)
- Large stirring spoon
- Water or vodka for the airlock (*see pic* 6, page 106)

Bottling

- Rubber siphoning tube
- 1½ pint glass bottles, either with cork, screwcap, or crown cap
- Corking or crown-capping machine, optional

Rhubarb wine

Rhubarb is a great ingredient to use for your first winemaking adventure since it is the first "fruit" (technically a vegetable) of the year to ripen and is so easy to make. Young rhubarb yields a pretty pink potion, but if you grow your own, it's also a great way to use up any tougher, stringy sticks.

This page: Rhubarb Wine and Apple Wine (left, behind)

How to make rhubarb wine

Makes 1 gallon

3 lb 5 oz rhubarb, wiped with a damp cloth, trimmed and cut into short lengths, say 1 1/4 inch

Finger of fresh ginger root, bruised

Thinly pared zest and juice of 1 lemon

1 gallon boiling water

For every pint (16 fl oz) of juice obtained, add 1 1/2 cups granulated sugar

You will also need

Large earthenware crock or stainless-steel preserving pan, 2 1/2 gallon capacity

Jelly bag or fine sieve

1 gallon sterilized demijohn/carboy

9 x 1 pint (16 fl oz) or 6 x 1 1/2 pint (24 fl oz/75 cl) sterilized glass bottles, with screwcaps, swing-tops, or corks (see box, page 13)

Put the rhubarb in an earthenware crock or stainless-steel pan, crushing it thoroughly with a wooden mallet or the end of a rolling pin (*see pic* 1).

Add the ginger, lemon zest, and juice. Pour the boiling water over the crushed fruit and stir well (*see pic* 2). Cover with a clean cloth that's weighted at the corners so it doesn't fall into the liquid, and leave for 10 days (*see pic* 3). Stir daily to ensure no mold forms on the surface.

Strain the liquid into another deep bowl or pan using a jelly bag or fine sieve (*see pic* 4). Add the sugar and stir until dissolved (*see pic* 5). Transfer to a demijohn/carboy. Cover the opening of the demijohn with a clean cloth, folded over several times like a fan (*see pic* 6), and leave for 10 days to ferment. If this does not happen naturally, add yeast (see box, page 84) and leave for another 24 hours.

Bung the demijohn securely, then leave in a cool, dark place for 12 months. Siphon into sterilized bottles. Follow the Country Wine Code, Still Wines route, page 86.

Making & keeping: Make in early spring, or for as long as rhubarb is in season. It can be drunk straight away or will keep for up to a year after bottling.

3
4

5

6

Apple wine

Makes 1 gallon

6 lb 10 oz apples, ideally windfall

1 1/4 gallons water

3 lb 5 oz granulated sugar

Rind of 1 lemon

5 oz raisins, chopped

You will also need

Crock or large deep bowl

Food mill (Mouli-legume) or grinder, optional

1 gallon sterilized demijohn/carboy

9 x 1 pint (16 fl oz) or 6 x 1 1/2 pint (24 fl oz/75 cl) sterilized glass bottles, with screwcaps, swing-caps, or corks (see box, page 13)

Apples can be made into wine in one of two ways. Either using the Country Wine Code method with fresh apples as here, or from juice, as illustrated on page 109. Raisins are used for sweetness (see Top Tips box, page 85).

Chop up or grind the apples and put into a crock or large, deep bowl. Add 2½ quarts of boiling water, cover with a clean cloth, and leave for 10 days. Stir twice daily.

Pour the mixture through a fine sieve. Transfer the liquid to a demijohn/carboy and return the pulp to the bowl.

Put the remaining 2½ quarts of water in a pan over medium heat, add the sugar, stir until dissolved, and add the lemon rind. Observe the level in the pan, increase the heat, and boil for 30 minutes, adding extra water to restore the original level as necessary. Pour this over the pulp and mash with a wooden spoon.

Transfer the pulp to a fine sieve set over a bowl. Once the strained juices have cooled a little, add them to the original juice in the demijohn/carboy. Add the chopped raisins. If the wine does not ferment naturally, add yeast (see box, page 84) and leave for another 24 hours. Follow the Country Wine Code, Still Wines route (page 86).

Making & keeping: Make in late summer and autumn and keep for 6 months before bottling. In spring, your wine will be ready to drink and won't improve with keeping.

Clover flower or dandelion wine

The absolute epitome of country wine! Made with just the pink flower heads of clover or the yellow petals of the dandelion flower gathered on a sunny afternoon, with the addition of yeast.

Makes 1 1/2 quarts

2 lb 3 oz clover flower heads or dandelion petals

3 pints boiling water

1/2 orange, 1/2 lemon thinly sliced

1 lb 2 oz granulated sugar

Small piece of root ginger

1 tsp fresh baker's yeast

You will also need

Large earthenware crock or bowl

jelly bag

4 pint fermentation jar

3 x 1 pint (16 fl oz) or 2 x 1 1/2 pint (24 fl oz/75 cl) sterilized glass bottles, with stoppers, screwcaps, or corks (see page 13)

Sterilize all the equipment (see box, page 13). Pull the petals from the flower heads, discarding all the green parts. Put them in the crock or large, deep bowl. Add the boiling water and cover with a clean cloth, securing the corners with clothespins to keep the cloth from falling into the liquid (*see pic* 3, page 91). Leave for 3 days at room temperature, stirring at least twice a day.

Add the orange and lemon slices and stir again. Leave for 7 more days, covered with the cloth, and stir at least twice each day. After this time, pour the steeped petals and water through a scalded jelly bag suspended over a large bowl and leave to drip. Pour the liquid into a saucepan and add the sugar. Add the ginger, bring to a boil, then simmer for 30 minutes, adding more water as the level reduces to restore it to the original level in the pan.

Strain again. When cooled until lukewarm, add the baker's yeast to the juice and pour into a sterile, 4 pint fermentation jar. Cover with a folded cloth (*see pic* 6, page 91). Follow the Country Wine Code, Still Wines route (page 86).

Making & keeping: Make in the summer and keep for 2 years before drinking, although if you can keep it for 4 years it is superb.

Note: Other edible flowers such as coltsfoot, elderflower, gorse, hawthorn, honeysuckle, pansy, and scented roses can be used to make flower wine.

Sweet raisin & flower wine

The inspiration for this floral recipe, which relies on the natural yeasts present in the air for fermentation, comes from the 16th edition of *The Compleat Housewife*. Choose aromatic flowers such as roses, jasmine, elderflower, or lavender, or experiment with dried flowers.

Makes 1 1/2 quarts

1 lb 10 oz fragrant flowers or rose petals, freshly picked

3 pints filtered or spring water

10 1/2 oz whole raisins, rinsed

You will also need

Deep bowl, jelly bag

4 pint sterile "demi"-demijohn/carboy

3 x 1 pint (16 fl oz) or 2 x 1 1/2 pint (24 fl oz/75 cl) sterilized glass bottles, with stoppers, screwcaps, or corks (see page 13)

Put the flowers or petals in a large, deep bowl. Boil the water and pour it over the petals. Cover with a clean cloth, weigh it down, with clothespins (*see pic* 3, page 91), and leave until the next day. Add the raisins and stir twice daily, morning and evening, for 12 days. Pour the liquid through a scalded jelly bag suspended over a large bowl. Leave to drip overnight, or until the dripping ceases.

Pour the liquid into a large jug and decant into the "demi"-demijohn/carboy. Cover the neck with a folded cloth or loosely fitted bung (*see pic* 6, page 91). If the wine does not ferment naturally, add yeast (see box, page 84) and leave for another 24 hours. Follow the Country Wine Code, Still Wines route (page 86).

Making & keeping: Make in the summer, drink after 12 months or (even better) after 2 years.

Note: If you see mold start to form, you've left it a little too long without stirring. Simply stir it well—the acid in the fruit will deal with the mold—but try to remember to stir more regularly. Keep covered with a cloth.

Gooseberry & star anise wine

I have always appreciated the humble gooseberry for its unique flavor in an old-fashioned pie or other traditional summer dessert, but it wasn't until I started making wines that I discovered that it has some pretty remarkable characteristics. Like the elderflower, it carries abundant natural yeasts to make sparkling drinks and wines without adding anything other than sugar and water.

Makes 3 to 4 quarts

3 quarts cold water, filtered where possible

1/4 cup granulated sugar

2 star anise

2 lb 3 oz ripe gooseberries

2 cups of granulated sugar for 1 quart of juice

You will also need

Large shallow dish

Crock or very large bowl

Scalded jelly bag

1 gallon sterilized demijohn/carboy

4 or 5 x 1 1/2 pint (24 fl oz/ 75 cl) sterilized bottles, preferably glass, with screwcaps or corks (see box, page 13)

Put the water in a large pan, add the sugar and the star anise, and bring to a boil. Simmer for 1 hour, then leave the sugar solution to cool.

Trim the tops and bottoms of the gooseberries with a pair of sharp scissors. Rinse, dry, and put in a large, shallow dish. Crush with the end of a rolling pin, add 3 pints of the cooled sugar solution and leave for 1 day, covered with a clean cloth.

Strain through a scalded jelly bag suspended over a crock or very large bowl and leave to drip overnight or until the dripping ceases.

For every 1 quart of juice extracted, add 2 cups of sugar, mix well and leave for 12 hours or until it starts to ferment (froth). If this doesn't happen, add yeast (see box, page 84) and leave for another 12 hours.

Skim off any surface debris that may have formed and transfer to a sterile demijohn/carboy with a loose bung or folded towel covering the opening (*see pic* 6, page 91). Let it stand for a month.

After this time, siphon the liquid into another sterile vessel to give it more air. Rinse the old demijohn/carboy with some of the gooseberry liquid, then return all the mixture to the original jar, seal and leave for 4 months before bottling.

When ready to bottle, rinse out the sterile bottles with warm water, fill with the liquid, leaving a small gap of ¾ inch between the top of the liquid and the top of the bottle. Screw down the cap firmly.

Making & keeping: Make in June and July, store for 4 months before bottling and drink immediately or keep for up to 12 months.

Beet & marjoram wine

Beets make a crystal-clear, dark-red wine. It can have an earthy taste that isn't for everyone, but adding hops bought from brewing shops and sweet herbs such as marjoram, thyme, or rosemary adds bouquet and produces a more amenable wine. Make this wine when the herbs are in flower in late summer; they are more fragrant then.

How to make beet & marjoram wine

Makes 1 1/2 quarts

3 lb 5 oz young beets; don't use old woody ones; otherwise the wine will taste earthy

2 quarts water

1 large bunch of marjoram in flower

5 g dried hop flowers

1 1/2 cups turbinado sugar

2 tsp fresh baker's yeast

1 thick slice of bread

You will also need

2 quart sterilized fermentation jar or "demi"-demijohn/carboy with bung

3 x 1 pint (16 fl oz) or 2 x 1 1/2 pint (24 fl oz/75 cl) sterilized bottles, preferably glass, with screwcaps or corks

Wash and scrub the beets to remove any soil, put in a large pan, and cover with the cold water (*see pic* 1). Add the marjoram and bring to a boil. Reduce the heat and simmer for 30 minutes. Add the hops and cook for another 10 minutes (*see pic* 2).

Leave to stand for 2 hours and strain into a deep bowl (*see pic* 3). Reserve the beets, peel and enjoy. Dissolve the sugar in the beet juice by stirring, and leave until the liquid cools to a lukewarm temperature (*see pic* 4).

Toast the bread and spread with the yeast and, while the juice is warm, float the toast on top (*see pic* 5). Cover the bowl with a clean cloth, weigh down the corners with clothespins, and leave for 36 hours. Discard the toast and strain the juice into the fermentation jar (*see pic* 6). Follow the Country Wine Code, Still Wines route (page 86).

Making & keeping: Make in late summer. Store in the dark and open after 6 months. Drink young; this is not a keeper.

Note: This wine is made with the old-fashioned method of spreading the yeast on hot toast and floating it on the surface while the liquid is still warm. The yeast is slowly introduced to the wine, slowing the froth of the yeast and creating a more refined drink.

3

4

5

6

A modicum of modern science

The Country Wine Code recipes are made simply with fruit, water, and baker's yeast, produced just as they used to be made in stills and country cottage kitchens everywhere. The recipes in this section borrow from both the Country Wine Code and the contemporary winemaking methods covered in the Modern Wine Model.

Carrot wine

Makes 1 gallon

4 lb 7 oz large carrots, 2 lemons, 2 oranges

3 lb 14 oz turbinado sugar

1 gallon water

1 heaped tsp Super Wine Yeast Compound or 1 packet of wine yeast (see box, page 84)

You will also need

Large pan, muslin, crock or fermentation bucket with lid*, 1 or 2 airlocks*, bungs*, brown paper, 2 x 1 gallon demijohns/carboys

6 x $1\frac{1}{2}$ pint (24 fl oz/75 cl) sterilized glass bottles**

This excellent root-vegetable wine was once known as "carrot whiskey"—not because it tastes like whiskey, but because it is reputed to have the same kick. It's tempting to think that the longer you cook the vegetables, the more flavor they will release into the water, but it is important to cook them only until just tender and for no longer.

Sterilize all equipment and utensils before you start**.

Wash and scrub the carrots (do not peel) and leave in the sun or fresh air to dry. Put the whole carrots in a large pan and add 1 gallon cold water. Observe the level of the water in the pan. Bring to a boil and simmer for 20 to 25 minutes. While the carrots are cooking, slice the lemons and oranges and put them with the sugar in a crock or fermentation bucket*.

When the carrots are tender, add enough water to bring the liquid back up to its original level. Switch off the heat and strain the water onto the fruit and sugar in the crock or fermentation bucket. Reserve the carrots for eating or making soup. Stir the liquid well to dissolve the sugar. Leave to cool to a lukewarm temperature. Add the yeast and stir well.

Cover the crock with a cloth or the fermentation bucket with a lid and fit an airlock (*see pic* 6, page 107). Put it in a warm place and leave it to ferment for 15 days.

Strain through a muslin- or cheesecloth-lined colander before pouring into a sterile demijohn/carboy. Wrap in brown paper to help retain the color, then seal with a bung fitted with an airlock.

When the wine stops bubbling, rack into a second, sterile demijohn/carboy with a solid bung. Wrap in brown paper and store away from the light. Rack off into sterilized bottles with stoppers when ready to drink.

Making & keeping: Make in summer. This takes 20 to 30 days, and needs to be kept 12 months before bottling.

Note: Use this method to make wine with other root vegetables. For something quite different, try sweet potatoes.

Orange wine

Orange wine is simple to make using the pared zest and juice of the fruit. It makes a rich, orange-colored, marmalade-y tasting drink.

Makes 1 gallon

12 oranges

3 quarts cold water

1 quart boiling water

3 lb 5 oz granulated sugar

1 heaped tsp of Super Wine Yeast Compound or 1 packet of wine yeast (see box, page 84)

You will also need

Crock or fermentation bucket with lid, bung and 2 bubbling airlocks*

2 x 1 gallon demijohn/carboys

6 x 1½ pint (24 fl oz/75 cl) sterilized glass bottles**

Sterilize all equipment and utensils before you start**.

Thinly pare the orange rind of 12 oranges with a potato peeler, put in a crock or fermentation bucket, add the boiling water, and let it stand for 24 hours. Juice the oranges and reserve the juice.

Strain the water into a fermentation bucket. Add 3 quarts of water, the orange juice and the sugar. Stir well to dissolve the sugar.

Add the yeast, stir well, close the bucket, and fit a bubbling airlock (*see pic* 6, page 107). Stir well and leave in a warm place for 2 to 3 days for the fermentation to start.

Transfer to a demijohn/carboy and fit a bung with an airlock. When fermentation has stopped, rack the wine into a second demijohn/carboy with a solid bung. Siphon off into sterilized bottles after 1 year.

Making & keeping: Make when citrus fruit is good. Keep 12 months until it is time to bottle. Siphon into bottles and your wine is ready to drink.

** See Equipment box, page 87*

*** See Sterilization box, page 13*

Sweet nettle wine

Nettles are well-known for making nourishing soup, good tea, refreshing beer, and sexually arousing wines. Viagra watch out: there is a forager's alternative about! If you're gathering nettles where they may have been sprayed, make sure you rinse them in baby-bottle sterilizing liquid according to the instructions.

Makes 1 gallon

Enough nettle tops to fit into a 2 quart jug

1 gallon water

3 lb 14 oz granulated sugar

Juice and thinly pared rind of 2 lemons

Small lump of root ginger, bashed

1 heaped tsp of Super Wine Yeast Compound or 1 packet of wine yeast (see box, page 84)

You will also need

Crock or fermentation bucket with lid, bung and airlocks*
2 x 1 gallon demijohns/carboys

6 x $1^1/_2$ pint (24 fl oz/75 cl) sterilized glass bottles

Sterilize and rinse all winemaking equipment and utensils before use (see box, page 13). Put the nettle tops in a pan with 2 quarts of water, the bashed ginger, and the thinly pared lemon rind. Bring to a boil and simmer for 45 minutes. Strain and make up the quantity to 1 gallon with the remaining water.

Put the sugar in a crock or fermentation bucket, add the liquid and the lemon juice, and stir well to dissolve the sugar. When the liquid has cooled to a lukewarm temperature, add the yeast and stir again.

Cover with a clean cloth, tipped lid or lid with an airlock (*see pic* 6, page 106) and keep in a warm place. After 4 days, stir the must and transfer to a demijohn/carboy fitted with an airlock. When the wine stops fermenting, rack it off into a second demijohn/carboy with a solid bung (see Glossary, page 196).

Siphon off into sterilized bottles when ready to drink.

Making & keeping: Make in summer and keep in the demijohn/carboy for at least 3 months before bottling.

** See Equipment box, page 87*

White plum wine

Yellow plums make much better wine than red ones. Wine made with red plums can taste insipid, and many winemakers tend to add 7 oz of soaked barley to counteract this "thinness" and create more body. The enzyme pectolase is added before fermentation starts to prevent the high levels of pectin causing a cloudy wine.

Makes 1 gallon

3 lb 14 oz yellow plums

1 quart boiling water

3 quarts cold water

1 tsp pectolase (see Glossary*)

3 lb 5 oz granulated sugar

1 heaped tsp of Super Wine Yeast Compound or 1 packet of wine yeast (see box, page 84)

You will also need

Crock or fermentation bucket with lid, bung and airlocks

2 x 1 gallon demijohns/carboys

6 x 1½ pint (24 fl oz/75 cl) sterilized glass bottles

Sterilize and rinse all winemaking equipment and utensils before use (see box, page 13). Cut the plums in half; there's no need to remove the stones. Put them in the crock or fermentation bucket and crush with a potato masher or rolling pin.

Pour the boiling water on the fruit and leave for 24 hours, covered with a clean cloth or loose lid. Mash from time to time. Add the cold water and the pectolase and leave for another 48 hours before straining into a large saucepan.

Bring the liquid to the boil, pour it back into the crock or fermentation bucket, and add the sugar. Stir until dissolved. Leave to cool until lukewarm, then add the yeast and stir. Cover with a cloth or lid fitted with an airlock.

When the wine stops fermenting, which can be anything from 2 to 5 or 6 weeks, rack it off into a demijohn/carboy. When it clears completely, rack it into a clean demijohn/carboy with a solid bung (see Glossary*). Siphon into sterilized bottles after a year when ready to drink.

Making & keeping: Make in late summer, and keep for 12 months before bottling. Your wine is ready to drink.

** Glossary can be found on page 196*

The modern way

According to long-time country winemakers Jim and Jean Haines, commercially produced wines have led to a decrease in winemaking at home. While many think it sounds complex, I hope that this book and Jim and Jean's simple method below might persuade you otherwise.

The modern wine model

Before you start, cleanliness is vitally important every step of the way, so ensure you sterilize all your equipment (see box, page 13). And, to yield the highest juice levels, freeze the fruit first.

1. Put 2 lb 3 oz of defrosted fruit in a plastic fermentation bucket and crush with a potato masher or the end of a rolling pin.
2. Add 1 gallon of filtered water or juice (according to recipe). Wine made with non-filtered water can taste like chlorine. Add 1 Campden tablet (see Glossary*) crushed with 1 tsp of sodium metabisulphate and leave for 2 days.
   This stops the fermentation of the naturally occurring yeasts in the fruit, preparing the wine for the addition of the dried yeast powder.
3. Test with a hydrometer (see Glossary*). You are looking for a specific gravity (SG) reading of between 1070 to 1090, which will make a dry wine of around 9 to 11% abv. If necessary, adjust by adding sugar syrup (see box, page 108, Note, page 112) according to the SG and the recipe.
4. Make a yeast starter solution by putting the yeast powder in a small bottle with 1 tbsp of granulated sugar and 1/2 cup warm water. Put a stopper in the bottle temporarily and shake. Take out the stopper immediately and replace with a cotton ball. Leave for 1 hour, by which time the yeast solution should be fermenting vigorously.
5. Add the solution to the liquid and stir.
6. Cover the bucket with a lid fitted with an airlock (see Glossary*), and pour ½ to ¾ inch of water or vodka into the airlock to prevent bacteria or air from seeping back into the must. Put in a warm place and leave to work for 10 days. NB Check it regularly! Once fermentation starts, transfer the bucket to a warm room and set it on a large tray to catch any spills in case things gets vigorous.
7. After 10 days or so when the yeast has stopped working, strain the liquid through a muslin- or cheesecloth-lined colander into a recently sterilized bucket (see box, page 13).
8. Transfer to a demijohn/carboy—clear glass for white wine and brown/green for red wines to prevent discoloration. Alternatively, wrap a clear glass demijohn/carboy in brown paper for red wines. Fill up to the vessel's shoulder height, then plug the opening loosely with a cork bung with an airlock (see Glossary*) and leave until the liquid stops bubbling.
9. If a lot of sediment has formed in the base of the vessel, rack the wine (see Glossary*) into a second, sterile demijohn/carboy; otherwise it will make a "mousey"-tasting beverage. Top up the level with cooled, boiled water to within ¾ inch of the cork. Any more space than this will cause the wine to oxidize.
10. Ensure that fermentation has stopped completely by adding a Campden tablet and 1 tsp of sodium metabisulphate.
11. Leave the wine in the demijohn/carboy until it's ready to drink.
12. Once the demijohn/carboy is opened, the wine must be bottled immediately to prevent oxidization. Rack into sterilized bottles and cork or screw caps on tightly.

Mature whites for 6 months before drinking unless they are extra-special, in which case keep for another year. Red wines should be drunk between 1 and 2 years.

** Glossary can be found on page 196*

1

2

3

4

5

6

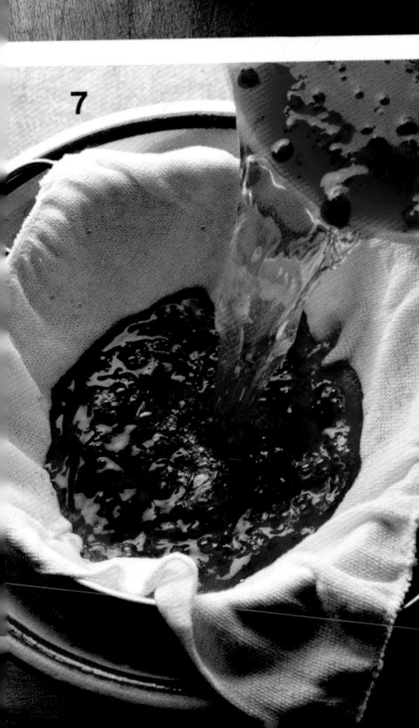
7

8

9

This page: Ingredients for Rosé Wine from Blackcurrants & Grape Juice

Sugar syrup

To make sugar syrup, dissolve 2 lb 3 oz granulated sugar in 1 pint (16 fl oz) boiling water. Make sure the sugar is completely dissolved then remove from the heat and leave to cool. Use as necessary.

Equipment

Crushing

- Wooden rolling pin or potato masher
- Colander, with muslin or cheesecloth to line

Fermentation

- Plastic fermentation buckets with lid, in sizes ranging from 1 to 6 gallons, either able to take an airlock or to be drilled to accept one
- Small bottle with stopper
- Small cotton ball
- Hydrometer
- Sterilization solution
- Sodium metabisulphate powder
- Campden tablets
- Several 1 gallon demijohns/carboys
- 2 bubbling airlocks
- Several bungs, both solid and drilled for bubbling airlocks
- Large stirring spoon
- Tray
- Sugar syrup (see box, opposite), made with granulated sugar
- Yeast powder to suit (see box, page 84), and sugar to make up starter yeast solution
- Water or vodka for the airlock

Storing & bottling

- Brown paper for red wines
- Sterilized 1½ pint glass bottles (24 fl oz/75 cl), with cork or screwcap closure (see box, page 13)

Rosé wine from blackcurrants & grape juice

Makes 1 gallon

14 oz frozen blackcurrants

2 quarts water, ideally filtered

1 quart white grape juice (not concentrate)

You will also need

Equipment as above

Sterilize all equipment and utensils before you start (see box, page 13).

Put the defrosted blackcurrants in a fermentation bucket and crush using the end of a rolling pin or potato masher. Add the water and grape juice and proceed as per the Modern Wine Model, Step 2 (see page 106).

Making & keeping: Make in the summer and drink within 12 months. Once open, consume immediately.

White apple wine from apple juice

Makes 1 gallon

1 gallon fresh apple juice

1 lb 2 oz raisins, chopped

You will also need

Equipment as above

Sterilize all equipment and utensils before you start (see box, page 13).

Put the fruit juice in a fermentation bucket; add the chopped raisins and continue as per the Modern Wine Model, Step 2 (see page 106).

Making & keeping: Make any time of the year. Store in the dark for 6 months before bottling. Does not improve with keeping.

Bully Lane red berry wine

Champion amateur winemaker Brian Fowler (see page 85) was a city boy when he married May and moved into her family home in Bully Lane. He lives there today with his son's family, where he makes this and many other wines. It can be made with a mixture of red berries or currants.

Makes 1 gallon

2 quarts filtered water

2 lb 3 oz frozen berries and/or currants

1 pint sugar syrup (see box, page 108)

1 quart red grape juice (not concentrate)

You will also need

Modern Wine Model equipment (see box, page 109)

Sterilize all equipment before you start (see box, page 13).

Defrost the berries and put them in the fermentation bucket. Crush the berries using the end of a rolling pin or potato masher. Add the water and grape juice and proceed as per the Modern Wine Model, Step 2 (see page 106).

Making & keeping: Drink after 3 months, but this improves after keeping for 12 months or more.

Note: When using elderberries, in order to reduce the high levels of tannin in the fruit, Brian recommends covering them with boiling water and straining them 2 or 3 times before steeping. Blending different varieties of berries—you can use blackberries, blackcurrants, and sloes—also helps to reduce tannin, giving the wine a rounder feel than one made from a single variety.

Red & white grape wine

Making wine from grapes in a colder climate is a little more challenging than making other fruit or vegetable wines. The fruit is more acidic in northern climes and sugar needs to be added to achieve the right balance in all but the very warmest of years. While the novice might choose to wing it, for the seasoned winemaker, a hydrometer is useful to ensure there is sufficient sugar (see Note below). If you have a vine and an excess of grapes, then a fruit press will be invaluable, but for your first attempt, you can hand-squeeze the fruit, backing this up with my old trick of using a sturdy potato masher. Alternatively, you might just like to try making this recipe with fresh grape juice.

Makes 1 gallon

1 gallon fresh grape juice, either squeezed from black grapes for red wines and green grapes for white, or bought, but not from concentrate

Sugar syrup as required, (see box, page 108; see Note, right)

You will also need

Modern Wine Model equipment (see box, page 109)

Sterilize all equipment before you start (see box, page 13).

If using your own fruit, crush or squeeze the grapes to extract the juice.

If making rosé, leave the skins with the juice for a couple of days. For a red wine, leave the juice with the skins for up to 10 days. The longer the skins stay in the juice, the richer and darker the wine, but be warned: 10 days are sufficient.

For white wine, wrap the grapes in calico (your jelly bag will do) or some other sturdy material when crushing.

Pour the juice into the fermentation bucket and proceed as for the Modern Wine Model, Step 2 (see page 106), checking and adjusting the sweetness of your must, if necessary, in stages (see Note below). You are looking for a specific gravity of 1090.

Making & keeping: Drink white and rosé after 6 months, but red improves after keeping for 12 months or more.

Note: With the Modern Wine Model, you will obtain a specific gravity (SG) of between 1070 and 1090. If your must falls below this, adding 2½ fl oz of sugar syrup will raise the SG by roughly 5. However, if you need to add more than 3½ fl oz, it is best to add in several instalments; 24 hours after the first sugar syrup has been added, check your must's SG again. If you need more, add another 3½ fl oz and stir. Test again the following day, adding extra syrup until the desired SG is reached. If the SG goes too high, dilute the must with cooled boiled water.

Fortified wines

Small amounts of brandy or other high-alcohol spirits enhance a wine's flavor while larger amounts inhibit the yeast and therefore halt fermentation. The resulting drink can therefore be bottled and left to mature after six days or so.

Fortified berry wine

This can be made with a mix of blackberries, blackcurrants, raspberries, and elderberries.

Makes 2 quarts

Enough mixed berries to fill a 1 quart measuring jug

2 quarts water, preferably filtered

1 3/4 cups granulated sugar for every 1 quart of juice

3 or 4 cloves and 1/2 tsp ground ginger

1 heaped tsp Super Wine Yeast Compound or 1 packet of wine yeast

5 fl oz brandy for every quart of wine

You will also need

Country Wine Code equipment (see page 87)

Crock or 2 quart "demi"-demijohn/carboy

2 x 1 quart (32 fl oz) sterilized glass bottles, with screwcaps, swing-caps, or corks

Sterilize all equipment before you start (see box, page 13).

Put the berries in a large pan, add the water, bring to a boil, and simmer for 30 minutes. Using the back of a spoon, press the fruit through a sieve into a large bowl.

Measure the juice and, for every quart of juice, add 1 3/4 cups granulated sugar. Stir well until dissolved. Return the sweetened juice to the pan, add the cloves and ground ginger. Gently bring to a boil, simmer for 15 minutes, then leave to cool.

Pour into a crock, fermentation bucket, or "demi"-demijohn/carboy and add "enough yeast to work."

Follow the Country Wine Code, Still Wines route (page 86). Once fermentation has stopped, add 5 fl oz of brandy to each quart of wine, then bottle, seal, and store.

Making & keeping: Keep for 6 months and once open, drink immediately.

Country "port"

In days gone by, country winemakers added brandy or spices or both to juice to ensure a good, consistent flavor.

Makes 2 quarts

1 lb 2 oz cranberries

1 lb 2 oz haws (hawthorn berries)

10 1/2 oz whole raisins

2 1/4 quarts water, preferably filtered

2 lb 3 oz sugar

1/2 level tsp of Super Wine Yeast Compound or 1 packet of wine yeast

5 fl oz brandy for every quart of wine

You will also need

Deep crock

Fermentation bucket, lid, bung and airlock

Clean cloth

Jelly bag, scalded

1 x 2 quart "demi"-demijohn/carboy

2 x 1 quart (32 fl oz) sterilized glass bottles, with screwcaps, swing-caps, or corks

Sterilize all equipment before you start (see box, page 13). Put the fruit in a crock or fermentation bucket. Crush with a potato masher or the end of a rolling pin.

Boil the water and pour it over the mashed fruit. Cover with a clean cloth or a loose lid and leave for 5 days, mashing every day.

Strain through a scalded jelly bag and leave to drip over a deep container or fermentation bucket. Add the sugar and stir well. Add the yeast, put in a warm place, cover with a tipped lid or a sealed lid with an airlock (see Glossary, page 196), and leave for 2 days, or until fermentation starts. Bring back to room temperature and leave to ferment for 6 more days.

Siphon into the "demi"-demijohn/carboy. Add the brandy. When fermentation stops, bottle according to the Country Wine Code (see page 86). If fermentation continues, add a little extra brandy. Seal, store, and keep.

Making & keeping: Open after 6 months; improves with keeping.

Variation: Try making this with damsons and other stone or foraged fruit. If you don't have access to haws, try with other fruits, or use all cranberries.

And now for something stronger

Liqueurs, digestifs & pick-me-ups

Liqueurs, digestifs & pick-me-ups

Making liqueurs is simple and rewarding. You put the ingredients together and time does the rest. There is no equipment or sterilization to worry about, and the results are always good. There isn't a better method of capturing the seasons in a bottle and what better way of finishing a meal than putting a decanter or bottle of something rich and delicious of your own making on the table to offer to friends?

In summer you can make liqueurs with just about any fruit—berries, cherries, plums, damsons, peaches, and citrus fruit—but you can use edible flowers, spices, nuts, coffee, chocolate, and seeds to make amazing concoctions, too. You can make your own cream liqueurs by adding cream to the liqueur before bottling. There is only one drawback: buying branded base spirits such as gin, whiskey, rum, or vodka means liqueur-making is an expensive business. But it can be a great way of using up that bottle of spirits you brought back from vacation and never drank. In countries where liqueur-making is traditional it is possible to buy inexpensive 90% abv spirit for just this purpose. Sadly, this option isn't available everywhere, but if you get into-liqueur making it is a good thing to bear in mind.

Most homemade liqueurs are made by steeping fruit, spices, flowers, herbs, citrus zest, or other ingredients in spirit for weeks on end, adding sugar, and then filtering and bottling. Many recipes also include citric acid, and although I do sometimes add it, I have not found it serves any useful purpose over and above the citrus zest.

Damson and sloe (the wild equivalent) gin have always been popular in the UK for staving off the winter cold and creating an inner glow. In southern Italy everyone who has a lemon tree in their garden (or even just in a pot on a terrace) makes their own Limoncello to offer their guests after dining al fresco. In the north, where the weather is more wild and stormy, you're more likely to be offered a homemade grappa flavored with cumin or fennel seeds.

The choices are almost endless. It is up to you to create your own tradition by creating a liqueur with something that grows in your garden, or that you have foraged while out on a country walk.

Bourbon shrub

"Shrub" and "bounce" are traditional generic names for certain types of after-dinner drinks and tonics made with fruit. Bounce is most commonly applied to stone-fruit concoctions, while shrub is reserved for citrus fruit. It is the simplest of liqueurs to make—you just put all the ingredients in a jar. As usual there is a bit of shaking and waiting to do. Make this shrub with lemons, limes, or grapefruit and experiment with other spirits.

Makes 1½ pints

1 pint bourbon

Finely grated zest of 2 unwaxed oranges and 1 lime

1 cup superfine sugar

You will also need

1 to 2 quarts clean, dry wide-necked preserving jar

Fine muslin or paper coffee filter

1 x 1½ pint (24 fl oz/75 cl) clean, dry bottle, or a selection of small bottles, with stoppers

Put the bourbon, citrus zest, and sugar into the wide-necked jar, seal and leave out of direct sunlight for 30 days, shaking 2 to 3 times daily.

After this time, open the jar and strain through a funnel lined with muslin or filter paper into a measuring jug and pour into the bottle(s) and seal. Ideally this should be kept for 3 months in a cool, dark cupboard before opening.

Making & keeping: Make when citrus fruit is at its best. Keeps indefinitely.

Opposite: Limoncello San Vigilio

Old Williamsburg mandarin tea

This punch recipe from *The Williamsburg Art of Cookery* is described as an "old Williamsburg recipe." It advises, "Fill the glasses with crushed ice when used. It will keep bottled." I decided to try it out and, believe me, it's a pretty strong tea, and without ice it makes a good after-dinner drink. Even if not strictly a liqueur, this is for impatient liqueur-makers who want a drink to make and consume immediately, although it improves with age.

Makes 1 quart

1 cup strong tea, cooled

Juice and rind of 2 mandarins

Juice of 1 extra mandarin

Juice and thinly pared rind of 1 lemon

2/3 cup turbinado or granulated sugar

1 3/4 cups top-quality rum

You will also need

2 x 1 quart (32 fl oz) clean, dry bottles, with stoppers

Start by scraping the pith off the back of the mandarin rind, then put all the ingredients in a bottle and close the cap. Shake well until the sugar dissolves. Leave overnight and strain through a sieve lined with muslin into a second bottle. Drink when the spirit moves you.

Making & keeping: Make in winter when mandarins are plentiful. Keeps for 6 months or more.

Variation: The original Williamsburg version used the thinly pared rind and juice of 2 lemons instead of mandarins; if you would like to try this, add a little more sugar to taste.

Illustrated on page 119

Limoncello San Vigilio

We associate Limoncello with Campania and the Amalfi coast in southern Italy, but my recipe was inspired by a magnificent and ancient lemon tree in the garden of Villa San Vigilio on Lake Garda in the north, where I was a guest many, many years ago. The dinner conversation turned to the stupendous lemon tree and I asked if they made Limoncello—which of course they didn't: this was grappa territory. However, one of the dinner guests was from Naples and kindly sent me this recipe by Neapolitan cook Fabrizia Gerli.

Makes 1 1/2 pints

4 unwaxed lemons

1 lime

1 3/4 cups gin, white rum or 95% abv liqueur spirit

3/4 cup granulated sugar

1 pint water

You will also need

1 to 2 quart clean, dry, wide-necked preserving jar

Fine muslin or paper coffee filter

1 x 1 1/2 pint (24 fl oz/75 cl) clean, dry bottle, with stopper

Pare the citrus zest thinly with a potato peeler, making sure there is no pith attached. Put the zest in a large jar, add your spirit of choice, seal the jar, and leave it in the dark for 7 to 10 days.

After this time make a syrup by boiling the sugar and water in a saucepan for 6 to 7 minutes. Leave to cool, then add the lemon-scented spirit.

Measure and strain through a funnel lined with muslin or filter paper into a measuring jug, pour into the bottle, and seal. Store in the dark for 1 week, then it's ready to drink. It is traditional to serve Limoncello frosted from the freezer. Try alternatives using oranges (Orangello), limes, or grapefruit.

Making & keeping: Make when lemons are at their best. Keeps indefinitely.

Nocino—Italian walnut liqueur

Nocino is made all over Italy where walnuts flourish, but this classic version is from Emilia-Romagna, where the liqueur is said to have originated. In Italy, tradition has it that the walnuts are picked in the early morning while still covered in dew on June 24, St John the Baptist's Day. I have heard herbal experts say that each healing plant has some visual characteristic that gives a clue to its medicinal qualities. For example, the nodding head of cowslip suggests it might be good for a headache. Nocino is rated highly in Italy for its digestive qualities; think of the complex, convoluted form of a walnut and it reminds us of the tangle of our intestines.

Makes 1 quart

30 green walnuts

1 quart aquavit, grappa, or other white spirit, such as vodka

Small piece of lemon zest

5 cloves

2 pieces broken cinnamon stick

1 lb 2 oz granulated sugar

You will also need

Rubber gloves—esssential to avoid black staining on nails and hands

3 quart clean, dry, wide-necked preserving jar

Fine muslin or jelly bag

1 x 1 quart (32 fl oz) clean, dry bottle or a selection of small bottles, with stoppers

1

2

Using gloves, cut the green walnuts into quarters and put in the wide-necked preserving jar. Add the spirit, lemon zest, cloves, and cinnamon. Seal the jar and leave on a sunny windowsill for 4 weeks; shake daily to clear any sediment from the bottom (*see pic* 1).

Open the jar and add the sugar, reseal it, and put back in the sun. Shake daily for 2 more weeks, or until the sugar has dissolved. Strain through a sieve lined with a piece of fine muslin or a jelly bag (*see pic* 2).

Measure the volume, and using a funnel, pour into the bottle(s), seal, and keep for Christmas.

Making & keeping: Make in early summer. Keeps indefinitely.

Green walnuts

When you cut open a green walnut, it is white inside and bleeds transparent juices. These quickly turn black when exposed to air, making a dark and delicious potion to drink after dinner, or to add to a tiramisu. Walnuts should be picked in early summer, before the shells have had a chance to harden. To test, push a darning needle into a walnut—if it comes out the other side you can make Nocino. If the needle meets the resistance of the shell, you're too late!

The original recipe for this delicious drink comes from Alto Adige, a mountainous region of northern Italy riddled with gently sloping, tree-covered valleys, each with its own microclimate, habitat, and produce. The liqueur is made with green walnuts before the shell has hardened (see box, page 123) and enriched with chocolate and spices. Creating a cream liqueur is my own take on a traditional recipe.

Spiced walnut & chocolate cream liqueur

Makes 1 quart

1 lb 2 oz green walnuts

1 tbsp good cocoa powder

A few pieces of cinnamon stick;

3/4 inch piece of vanilla pod

1 1/2 cups grappa or aquavit

1/2 cup rum

1 1/4 cups granulated sugar

1 pint heavy cream

You will also need

Rubber gloves—esssential to avoid black staining on nails and hands

2 to 3 quart clean, dry wide-necked preserving jar

Jelly bag

1 x 1 quart (32 fl oz) clean, dry bottle, or a selection of small bottles, with stoppers

Using rubber gloves, wash and dry the walnuts, cut them in half, and put into the wide-necked preserving jar. Add the cocoa and cinnamon. Scrape out the seeds from the vanilla pod and add the seeds and pod to the jar. Add the spirits and seal the jar.

Position on a sunny windowsill and shake daily for 6 to 8 weeks. Do this thoroughly, because the cocoa and spices tend to stick to the bottom of the jar. It is important to keep shaking until the glass clears.

Strain the liquid through a jelly bag suspended over a large bowl and leave to drip overnight, or until the dripping ceases.*

Add the sugar, stirring until it has dissolved, then add the cream. Strain again through a fine sieve, measure the volume, and use a funnel to pour into the bottle(s). Seal and drink immediately, or keep refrigerated.

If you want to keep this liqueur for Christmas, I suggest bottling it after the sugar has been added, then sealing. A few days before the festivities, pour it into a bowl, add the cream, strain, measure, and bottle again. Store in the refrigerator and drink immediately.

Making & keeping: Make in early summer. Drink immediately, unless you have enough willpower to wait until Christmas (see above).

* **Note:** To make the most of those leftover spice-infused walnuts, put them in a jar, cover with Marsala and seal. Serve after dinner with cheese, or in a glass of Marsala. They have a wonderful chocolatey flavor.

"Gin tonic"

This classic British county tipple was originally made in June with the frothy and fragrant, creamy-white elderflowers found in hedges and waste ground the length and breadth of the country. I have adapted the recipe to use other fragrant edible blooms such as rose petals, lavender, and orange blossom. The original recipe used brandy, but vodka would work, too. I have used gin, and though extravagant I prefer Williams Chase Elegant Crisp Gin from Herefordshire (on my doorstep), but you should use your own favorite brand.

Makes 1 pint

1/4 cup honey

1 cup dessert wine

3 handfuls fresh elderflowers, rose, lavender, jasmin, geranium, or orange blossom petals or a mixture

1 vanilla pod

1 1/4 cups gin (Williams Chase Elegant Crisp or an alternative top-quality gin)

You will also need

2 to 3 quart clean, dry wide-necked preserving jar

Jelly bag

1 x 1 pint (16 fl oz) clean, dry bottle, with stopper

Lightly warm the honey and mix with the wine, then leave to cool.

Put the flowers or petals in a shallow bowl and add the honey and wine mixture.

Split open the vanilla pod, scrape out the seeds, and add the pod and seeds to the bowl. Cover with a clean cloth and leave for 3 days.

Transfer to a large preserving jar and add half the gin (or other spirit, if using), stir well, and leave for 6 to 7 weeks.

Strain the liquid through a jelly bag suspended over a large bowl and leave to drip overnight, or until the dripping ceases. Measure the volume and use a funnel to pour into the bottle(s). Top up with the remaining spirit and seal. Store in the dark for a few months before drinking.

Making & keeping: Make in summer. Mature in bottle until Christmas. Keeps indefinitely.

Summer in a bottle

This may sound sickly sweet, but believe me: it isn't! Drink it neat after dinner, or pour it over ice and top with sparkling water as a refreshing summer aperitif—and don't forget to float a few fresh flower petals on top.

Cherry brandy

Disappearing into the cool embrace of the leafy, fruit-laden branches of a cherry tree on a hot summer's day holds a pleasure all of its own. I remember picking cherries as a child in a cottage garden in Herefordshire and the thrill of delivering the basket of plump fruit back home. Since those far-off days I have visited cherry orchards in Italy and France, and I only have to close my eyes, bite into a cherry, and I am back in that tree.

Makes 1½ pints to 1 quart

1 lb 2 oz ripe cherries

1¼ to 1½ cups granulated sugar

Small piece of orange zest

1 pint brandy

1¼ cups to 1 pint heavy cream, to taste (see Cherry Cream Liqueur variation, below), optional

You will also need

2 quart clean, dry wide-necked preserving jar

Jelly bag

1 x 1½ pint (24 fl oz/75 cl)—or if adding cream, 1 x 1 quart/32 fl oz—clean, dry bottle, or a selection of small bottles, with stoppers

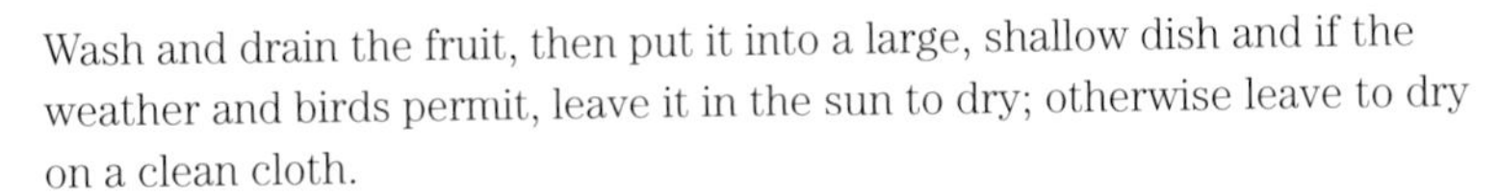

Wash and drain the fruit, then put it into a large, shallow dish and if the weather and birds permit, leave it in the sun to dry; otherwise leave to dry on a clean cloth.

Break up the fruit with a potato masher. Take a handful of cherry stones and smash them using a pestle and mortar to release the kernels.

Put the fruit, kernels, and the crushed stones in the wide-necked preserving jar and add the sugar and orange zest. Add the brandy, seal the jar, and leave it in the sun, either outside or on a windowsill, for 6 weeks. Shake the jar thoroughly every day.

Strain the liquid through a jelly bag suspended over a large bowl and leave to drip overnight, or until the dripping ceases. Measure the volume and use a funnel to pour into the bottle(s) and seal. Store in the dark and enjoy at Christmas.

Making & keeping: Make in early summer. Mature in bottle for 5 months. Keeps indefinitely.

Variation: To make Cherry Cream Liqueur, add the cream to the strained liqueur, mix well, strain again, and bottle as normal. Over time the liqueur and cream will separate; simply shake the bottle. It's ready to drink immediately. Store in the refrigerator and it will keep for a couple of months.

Right: Cherry Brandy (left) and Cherry Cream Liqueur

Quantities & bottling

It is always difficult to judge just how much finished liqueur you're going to end up with. While the fruit is macerating in the sun, the spirit evaporates. Always measure the volume after straining, then choose bottles to suit. And try to fill the bottle rather than leaving space at the top. Choose a single large bottle or a selection of smaller ones to give as gifts. Note: 24 fl oz or 75 cl is the size of a standard wine bottle.

Mrs Beeton's "fast cherry wine"

British recipe icon Mrs Beeton called this recipe Cherry Wine, which to our ears is confusing, since wine is not a liqueur and doesn't contain spirit. Yet any wordsmith will tell you that our language is constantly evolving, not only in terms of idioms and expressions but in the actual meaning of words—and this is doubly true when it comes to drinks. We would never expect a tonic or a cordial to be alcoholic, or a wine to have spirit in it. However, Mrs Beeton and her contemporaries certainly did. It's rather like the modern use of the word "beverage" to describe a beer—in my youth, "beverages" were an alcohol-free zone!

Makes 1 pint

For every 1 pint of cherry juice obtained:

4 1/2 oz sugar cubes

Scant pinch of ground mace, allspice, and cloves

1/2 cup brandy

1/2 cup dark rum

You will also need

Food mill (Mouli-legume)

1 x 1 pint (16 fl oz) clean, dry bottle or a selection of small bottles, with stoppers

Note: The amount of fruit is deliberately not given because the recipe depends on the amount of juice obtained from it. The fruit is cooked whole with the stones, then the stones are discarded. The juice yield can fluctuate according to evaporation and the size of the stones. A rough guide is: 2 lb 3 oz of fruit will yield 1 cup of juice and 1 pint of liqueur; but if making this recipe with plums or damsons, the yield will be very different.

Put the cherries in a heatproof bowl over a saucepan of simmering water. Cook gently until the juice runs freely. This may take up to an hour.

Transfer the fruit to a food mill set over a bowl. Extract as much juice as possible, then strain the juice through a sieve lined with muslin and measure the volume. If you don't have a food mill use a strainer and the back of a spoon (but this is time- and energy-consuming).

Pour the juice into a large saucepan, add the sugar and spices, and boil for a few minutes. Then strain again through a sieve lined with muslin and add the spirits; use a funnel to pour into the bottle(s) and seal.

Making & keeping: Make in midsummer. Ready to drink immediately. Keeps indefinitely.

Herefordshire vet—aromatic fruit liqueur

Think blackcurrants, think cassis, and think what wonderful concoctions you can make with them! I found this handwritten recipe tucked away in the Herefordshire Records Office in a notebook kept by a 19th-century country vet, along with all kinds of helpful hints for tending livestock. The original drink was made with wild elderberries, which make an equally delicious liqueur, but you can use any kind of edible wild berry growing near to where you live. The addition of the fennel was my own personal twist. When I was making this in July, the fennel bushes in my garden were covered in tiny yellow flowers. If you don't have fennel flowers, simply leave them out, but don't add fennel seeds because they would impart too strong a flavor. Use gin or vodka—whichever you prefer.

Makes 1 pint

7 oz blackcurrants, elderberries, rosehips, or other edible wild berries

2 whole cloves

6 juniper berries, crushed

1 tsp cumin seeds

2 heads of flowering fennel, optional

1 cup granulated sugar

1¾ cups gin or vodka

You will also need

Large shallow dish

Mortar & pestle

2 to 3 quart clean, dry, wide-necked preserving jar

Jelly bag

1 x 1 pint (16 fl oz) clean, dry bottle or a selection of small bottles, with stoppers

Wash the fruit and drain, then put into a large, shallow dish, and if weather permits, leave in the sun to dry; otherwise leave to dry on a clean cloth. Put the fruit in the mortar and crush with the pestle. Put the crushed fruit in a wide-necked preserving jar and add the spices and herbs, sugar, and the vodka or gin. Seal and leave for 3 weeks on a sunny windowsill. Shake daily to dissolve the sugar—this will take around 2 weeks.

Strain the liquid through a jelly bag suspended over a large bowl and leave to drip overnight, or until the dripping ceases. Measure the volume, use a funnel to pour into the bottle(s), and seal. Store in the dark for a month before drinking, but improves if kept for 6 months or more.

Making & keeping: Make in midsummer. Keeps indefinitely.

Patience makes perfect sense

Very little specialist equipment is needed for making liqueurs, but you do need patience. A large, wide-necked preserving jar is essential, and after six or eight weeks of shaking, the fruit has to be strained through a jelly bag or muslin cloth, then bottled. It is wise to label your jar with the date the liqueur was first started and the date when the next step will take place. Bottles don't need sterilizing; with so much sugar and alcohol, there's little chance of any bacteria taking hold. Simply wash bottles in hot, soapy water before use. Once bottled, label with the date of bottling and the date when the liqueur is best to drink. Patience is then required, since it is best to wait some months before opening to allow the liqueur to mature and reach its optimum state. Tradition has it that, like pickles and chutneys, you make liqueurs in summer, when the ingredients come into season, to keep and enjoy at Christmas.

Redcurrant & rosemary vodka

Redcurrants are such a beautiful fruit with a clear, rich color that makes perfect jellies and drinks. The long clusters of red, glass-like berries hang from the bush in profusion and in a good season make easy picking. The word "vodka" tends to conjure up the idea of a strong, harsh spirit, but this is far from the truth. Vodka makes wonderfully rounded fruit drinks and balances the sharpness of the fruit perfectly. I have added rosemary here to give extra bouquet; the aromatics comes through well. It would be well worth experimenting with thyme, mint, sage, majoram, and fennel—even an infusion of vodka and mixed herbs.

Makes 1½ pints

14 oz redcurrants

1 large sprig of rosemary

1 ¾ cups turbinado sugar

1 pint vodka

You will also need

2 to 3 quart clean, dry wide-necked preserving jar

Jelly bag

1 x 1½ pint (24 fl oz/75 cl) clean, dry bottle or a selection of small bottles, with stoppers

1

2

Wash and dry the currants. Using a fork, pull the currants off the stems. Put the fruit in a mortar with the rosemary and sugar and pound with the pestle (*see pic* 1). Cover with a clean cloth and leave overnight.

The following day, fill the wide-necked preserving jar with the crushed fruit and juices, then add the vodka (*see pic* 2). Seal and leave for 2 months on a sunny windowsill. Shake daily.

Strain the liquid through a jelly bag suspended over a large bowl and leave to drip overnight, or until the dripping ceases. Measure the volume and use a funnel to pour into the bottle(s) and seal. Store in the dark for 1 month before drinking.

Making & keeping: Make in midsummer. Keeps indefinitely.

Peach & vanilla vodka

Use this versatile recipe to experiment with tastes and the fruit you have to hand—use peaches, nectarines, apricots, or plums, or a mixture of fruit and personalize by adding your own spices. Try apricot and almond essence, nectarine and star anise, plum and cardamom. Replace vodka with gin or another white spirit to suit your taste buds. It's best to start this recipe early in the morning, but if this isn't possible, the pulp can be left covered overnight in a shallow dish, then placed in the sun the following day. If the sun is illusive, put it in the oven on the lowest setting with the door open for a few hours.

Makes 1 quart

1 lb 2 oz fruit (peaches, nectarines, apricots, or plums), stoned weight

1 vanilla pod

1 1/2 pint vodka or other spirit

1 1/2 cups granulated sugar

Pinch of citric acid

5 fl oz boiling water

You will also need

Shallow dish

Clean cloth

2 to 3 quart clean, dry wide-necked preserving jar

Jelly bag

1 x 1 1/2 pint (24 fl oz/75 cl) or 1 quart (32 fl oz) clean, dry bottle, or a selection of small bottles, with stoppers

Wash the fruit, cut it in half and remove the stones, reserving 3 of the stones. Put the fruit in a saucepan with just enough water to cover the base.

Crack open the reserved stones using a pestle and mortar to release the kernels; add the kernels to the pan. Cut open the vanilla pod, scrape out the seeds, and add the pod and seeds to the fruit.

Cover with a lid and cook gently until very soft—1 to 2 hours, depending on the ripeness of the fruit.

Reduce to a fine pulp with a potato masher, transfer to a shallow dish and leave in the hot sun for 8 hours covered with a cloth to keep off the flies.

After this time, transfer the pulp into the wide-necked preserving jar and add the spirit. Seal the jar and leave for 2 to 3 weeks. Shake once a day.

Dissolve the sugar in boiling water and leave to cool. Add the citric acid, then add the liquid to the fruit pulp and mix well.

Strain the liquid through a jelly bag suspended over a large bowl and leave to drip overnight, or until the dripping ceases. Measure the volume and use a funnel to pour into the bottle(s) and seal. Store in the dark and enjoy at Christmas.

Making & keeping: Make in high summer. Mature in bottle until Christmas. Keeps indefinitely.

Previous pages: Redcurrant & Rosemary Vodka (left) and Peach & Vanilla Vodka

Strawberry rum cordial

This recipe was born out of an overpowering desire to capture the essence of perfectly ripe, freshly picked, sweet-smelling strawberries. I make a lot of strawberry jam through the season and I'm always on the lookout for the perfect strawberry. Knowing this, my local fruit and vegetable man turned up on my doorstep one day with trays of the most beautiful strawberries ever—red to their very core. We ate some, I made some jam, and then I wondered what I should do with the rest....

Makes $1\frac{1}{2}$ pints

2 lb 3 oz firm ripe local strawberries, hulled and cut into quarters

$\frac{1}{2}$ cup granulated sugar

1 cup white rum

$1\frac{1}{2}$ pint bottle of sparkling wine or water, to serve

You will also need

Double boiler or bowl and saucepan

Jelly bag

1 x $1\frac{1}{2}$ pint (24 fl oz/75 cl) clean, dry bottle or a selection of small bottles, with stoppers

Put the strawberries in the top of a double boiler or in a bowl over a saucepan of water. Add the sugar and put over medium heat to bring gently to a boil (*see pic* 1). Half-cover with a lid, then simmer for around 30 to 45 minutes, until the juices start to flow.

Transfer the fruit and juice to a jelly bag, suspend over a bowl, and leave to drip overnight, or until the dripping ceases (*see pic* 2).

Measure the volume of juice (do not squeeze the bag; this causes the juice to go cloudy)—there should be around $1\frac{3}{4}$ cups to 1 pint. Leave to cool, and then add the white rum (*see pic* 3). Use a funnel to pour into the bottle(s), and seal.

To serve: pour $\frac{1}{3}$ Strawberry Rum Cordial to $\frac{2}{3}$ sparkling wine or water.

Making & keeping: Make in summer. Ready to drink immediately. Keeps 6 months before flavor and color starts to deteriorate.

Experiment!

It is very tempting to want to add more fruit to the spirit than tradition and recipes require. However, if you add too much fruit to spirit your liqueur will start to ferment and corks will blow. Always follow the quantities in the recipe. The area where you can experiment and make a departure from the recipe is in using different spirits, fruits, and flavors, but still keep to the quantities listed. You may like the sound of the Coffee Cream Liqueur (see page 144), for example, but prefer whiskey to rum, so make it with rum! You love the sound of the Strawberry Rum Cordial (see opposite) but have a tree full of mulberries; use those. As I say, make your liqueurs your own.

Damson gin

This is a traditional British drink, also made with sloes, that people living in the country have continued to make from generation to generation, despite the sophisticated swirls of drinking fashions. The damson is a small, cultivated, plum-like fruit; sloes are their wild cousins found growing in the hedges that line rural lanes. Both are autumnal fruits, and wild plums would work, too.

Makes 1 quart

1 lb 5 oz damsons (or sloes)

1 cup turbinado sugar

1 ½ pints gin

You will also need

2 to 3 quart clean, dry wide-necked preserving jar

Fine muslin or jelly bag

1 x 1 ½ pints (24 fl oz/75 cl) or 1 quart (32 fl oz) clean, dry bottle, or a selection of small bottles, with stoppers

1

2

Wash and drain the fruit, then put it into a large, shallow dish. If weather permits, leave it in the sun to dry; otherwise, leave to dry on a clean cloth.

Pierce the damsons with the fine prongs of a (preferably silver) fork (*see pic* 1), and put into a large, wide-necked preserving jar. Add the sugar and the gin (*see pic* 2), seal, and leave for 6 weeks, shaking the jar every day (*see pic* 3).

Pour the fruit through a sieve lined with fine muslin or jelly bag suspended over a bowl and leave to drip overnight, or until the dripping ceases (*see pic* 4). Measure the volume and use a funnel to pour into the bottle(s); (*see pic* 5). Seal. Keep until Christmas.

Making & keeping: Make in late summer, early fall. Mature in bottle until Christmas. Keeps indefinitely.

3

4

5

Right: Vanilla Brandy

Instant blackberry brandy

This warming fruit shot can be made using any of my cordial recipes (see pages 10 to 43), but I include the full recipe below. It doesn't require steeping or standing and can therefore be enjoyed immediately. Naturally, if you don't want to drink it all at once it will keep and stand the test of time, but it won't improve in flavor as others do. Drink hot or cold!

Makes 1 pint

14 oz blackberries, loganberries, or raspberries or a mixture

1 1/4 cups granulated sugar

1 1/2 cups water

Scant pinch of ground cloves

Good pinch of ground cinnamon and ginger

1/2 cup brandy

You will also need

Jelly bag

1 x 1 pint (16 fl oz) clean, dry bottle or a selection of small bottles, with stoppers

Put the fruit in the saucepan with half the sugar and ½ cup of water, add the spices, and bring to a boil. Turn down the heat and simmer for a few minutes.

Put the remaining sugar in a saucepan with ½ cup of water and bring to a boil. Stir and simmer gently for 5 minutes, or until reduced by one-third.

Combine the 2 syrups, then strain the liquid through a jelly bag suspended over a large bowl and leave to drip overnight or until the dripping ceases. Top up with ½ cup of boiling water. Leave to cool, then add the brandy. Measure the volume and use a funnel to pour into the bottle(s) and seal. Drink at your pleasure.

Making & keeping: Make in late summer, early autumn. Ready to drink immediately. Keeps for a month or so.

Vanilla brandy

Vanilla pods or any other whole spice can be added to brandy and sugar syrup to make a lovely mellow liqueur—perfect for after-dinner drinking, a warming midmorning "skeeters" (liqueur-laced coffee), or for adding to ice cream, pancakes, or poached fruit.

Makes 1 3/4 pints

1 vanilla pod

1 pint basic brandy

3/4 cup water

3/4 cups granulated sugar

You will also need

1 x 1 1/2 pints (24 fl oz/75 cl) or 1 quart (32 fl oz) clean, dry bottle, with stopper

Split the vanilla pod open and scrape out the seeds and then add them with the pod to the bottle of brandy. Sseal, shake, and leave in a dark, warm place for 2 weeks, then strain, reserving the vanilla pod. Put the water and sugar in a pan and bring gently to a boil. Stir well to dissolve the sugar, remove from the heat, and leave to cool, then add the brandy and stir. Measure the volume and using a funnel pour into a bottle and add the reserved vanilla pod. Seal and store in a dark, dry place and try and forget about it for 6 months to a year. The longer it's kept, the better the taste. Serve as above.

Making & keeping: Make any of the time. Keeps indefinitely.

Variation: Try cinnamon sticks, ginger root, star anise or other whole spices.

Venetian eggnog

Eggnog, or Vov as it is known in Italy, is a traditional Christmas drink in many parts of the world. The word *vov* comes from the Venetian dialect word for egg and is made like other eggnogs with milk or cream, egg yolks, brandy, and sugar. Vov, however, contains Marsala, making it a sort of liquid zabaglione. Traditionally it was stored in earthenware bottles; today it is kept in glass bottles in the refrigerator. Drink hot or cold.

Makes 1 1/2 quarts

1 vanilla pod

1 quart whole milk

6 egg yolks

1 1/4 cups granulated sugar

1 cup Marsala

5 fl oz brandy

You will also need

2 x 1 1/2 pint (24 fl oz/75 cl) clean, dry bottles, with stoppers

Slit open the vanilla pod, scrape out the seeds, and put the seeds and the pod in a pan with the milk. Bring gently to simmering point, whisking from time to time.

Put the egg yolks in a second pan with the sugar and the Marsala and beat well (*see pic* 1).

When the vanilla milk is hot but not boiling, stir it into the egg-yolk mixture (*see pic* 2).

Put the pan on medium heat and warm through gently, whisking all the while. Do not let the mixture boil; otherwise, it will curdle. The mixture is ready when it starts to thicken. If is shows any sign of curdling or separating, take off the heat and whisk hard.

Strain with a fine sieve into a pan or measuring jug (*see pic* 3), add the brandy, leave to cool, and bottle using a funnel.

Keep for 2 days before serving. Store in the refrigerator and shake well before pouring.

Making & keeping: Make any time of year, but it is most appreciated in winter. Keeps for 6 months or so.

Variation: The original Vov recipe is made with 90% abv liqueur spirit rather than brandy; if you try this, then increase the sugar by 1/2 cup.

You can also try a brandy-only version, using the same amount of brandy and omitting the Marsala, and topping with grated nutmeg.

Illustrated on page 145

Keeping

There is no need to store liqueurs in the refrigerator. They will keep indefinitely—well, at least as long as the contents of the bottle last and if they are kept cool, away from direct sunshine. It is best to store cream and egg liqueurs in the refrigerator. These do separate, so give the bottle a good shake before serving, and if they have been stored in the refrigerator remember to bring them back to room temperature before serving. If the neck of the bottle is especially narrow, it may get blocked and you will need to free it with a skewer.

1

2

3

Opposite: Venetian Eggnog (left) and Coffee Cream Liqueur

Adding cream to drinks

Cream can be added to any liqueur; you can use light, heavy, or even whipping cream. Heavy cream unsurprisingly gives the richest flavor, but it does tend to clog up the neck of the bottle. Light cream behaves really well, remaining runny to the last, but it doesn't make the liqueur taste or look quite as special as the thicker creams. Whichever cream you choose for your drink, you will need to store the bottle in the refrigerator if keeping long-term and bring it back to room temperature before serving, giving it a good shake before pouring.

Coffee cream liqueur

This is the perfect end to a meal. Add cream if you like a cream liqueur but leave it out if you prefer a stronger one. Make this liqueur anytime of year.

Makes 1 quart

1 lemon

6 oz fine ground coffee

1 pint rum

2 cups turbinado or granulated sugar

1 pint heavy or whipping cream

You will also need

1 to 2 quart clean, dry, wide-necked preserving jar

Fine muslin

1 x 1 quart (32 fl oz) clean, dry bottle, with stopper

Scrub the lemon and finely pare the rind with a potato peeler. Put it in the wide-necked preserving jar, add the coffee and the rum, and leave to stand for 1 week.

Add the sugar and shake well to dissolve it.

Leave for 7 more days, shaking twice daily.

Strain through a sieve lined with a piece of fine muslin into a bottle, seal, and leave for 3 months.

When ready to serve, add the cream to the bottle, shake, and serve.

Store in the refrigerator or in a cool place. Bring to room temperature and shake the bottle well before serving.

Making & keeping: Make any time of the year. Keeps indefinitely until cream is added. Once cream is added, it will keep for 6 months in the refrigerator.

Taking the plunge

Punches, cups & party drinks

Previous pages: Charlotte Rose (see page 155)

Punches, cups & party drinks

There is nothing more welcoming than the site of a punchbowl on a party table and the sound and sight of a ladle plunging into the liquid, stirring up the fruit, and scooping up a serving of delicious punch.

Hot or cold cups and punches are festive, traditional, and practical when large numbers of people are involved. They can be mixed in advance, and the sparkling elements added when ready to serve. For cold punches use chilled ingredients or an iceberg block (see box, page 161) instead of adding lots of ice, which will make the punch watery. Serve hot punches straight from the pan in the kitchen or from a small portable hotplate on your party table. Punchbowls, whether glass, ceramic, silver, or other metals, are beautiful and are the perfect receptacle, but they are not essential. Be creative; use a large pan or even a new large white plastic bowl or bucket and artfully disguise it using a pretty cloth or a festive box and some greenery or flowers. Use a ladle or small jug to serve.

Fresh fruit is the ingredient that makes a punch look inviting. You can use slices of citrus, tropical, and hard fruits, or add whole berries or pomegranate and passion fruit seeds. My tip is to soak the fruit in advance in the spirit with the sugar (if using) and add the other chilled ingredients when guests arrrive. Serve punches in wine glasses, rummers, or punch cups (small glasses with handles).

Beyond the fizz

It's tempting to reach for bottles of sparkling wine when making party drinks, but cider, perry, and beer make delicious festive punches, too. You can use your own homemade liqueurs to give depth of flavor and create something a little bit different. Fruit cordials add flavor and eye candy to the drink: Syrop de Grenadine is a classic, made with pomegranate seeds; Italian Lime Siroppo adds green; Florida Cocktail, orange; Rose Petal, pink; and Artusi's Siroppo di Frutta, red (see pages 10 to 43).

Old English cider cup

Punch recipes should be adaptable. I like to start this one off strong so that it has impact and then ease off on the spirit and increase the soda as the evening goes on. Make sure you put plenty of lemon juice on the apple wedges before they go into the punch to prevent them from turning brown. Ciders, like wines, vary in sweetness. If you like sweet, use this style but always taste your punch to check the flavor. It is easy to add a little extra sugar before serving if necessary. I recommend a sparkling cider for this recipe.

Serves 4 to 8

½ to 1 cup brandy (apple if possible), to taste

1 vanilla pod

2 tbsp superfine sugar, or more to taste depending on cider used

1 quart top-quality sparkling hard cider

1 to 1½ pints soda water, optional

1 thinly sliced lemon

1 dessert apple, unpeeled cut into wedges and tossed in lemon juice

You will also need

2½ to 3 quart punchbowl or large stainless-steel pan

Spirit measure

Using a spirit measure, add the brandy to a punchbowl or a large stainless-steel pan. Slit the vanilla pod, scrape out the seeds, and add to the brandy. Add the superfine sugar and leave for at least an hour, or until required.

When ready to serve, top up with the hard cider and 1 pint of soda and stir well. Taste and add extra sugar if necessary, and more soda as required. Add the fruit, stir again, and ladle into wine glasses or punch cups.

Mulled cider

On festive occasions when the weather gets cold I like to greet friends with a glass of this hot winter punch. It is a gloriously warming drink. Gather all the ingredients and make the punch in advance, cover, and then simply reheat when your guests arrive and add slices of apple to each glass. Heirloom apple varieties impart fragrance and flavor to the mulled cider.

Put the measured brandy, hard cider, cloves, cinnamon stick, lemon peel and juice, bitters, Ginger Cordial, and apples in the pan. Put over medium heat and leave to simmer very gently for 10 minutes (with the lid on). Make sure you don't break up the apples. Ladle while still hot into heatproof wine glasses or punch cups. To prevent a glass from cracking, put a teaspoon into it to conduct the heat away from the glass.

Serves 8 to 12

1/2 to 1 cup brandy

2 quarts dry, non-sparkling hard cider (see page 76)

12 whole cloves

Cinnamon stick

Thinly pared peel and juice of 2 lemons

Good shake of Angostura bitters

1/2 cup Ginger Cordial (see page 21) or wine

4 small red garden apples, thinly sliced, unpeeled

You will also need

Large copper pan or other large pan with fitting lid

Spirit measure

Heatproof wine glasses or punch cups

Normandy cider cooler

One of the discoveries I made on my visit to the Normandy cider producers was Normandy Pommeau (a blend of apple juice and Calvados). It appears on traditional menus in countless recipes, from desserts to sauces and foie gras. It is served chilled as an aperitif or dessert wine and is a universal offering to honor guests in homes and restaurants all over the region. It is not easily sourced outside of Normandy, but it is worth buying a bottle if you get the chance, because it is a delicious drink and an excellent cooking ingredient. Internationally famous Calvados producer Christian Drouin also produces Pommeau, and this may be your best way of tracking it down.

Serves 4 to 8

5 oz strawberries, sliced

2 small apples, unpeeled, sliced

1/2 cup Pommeau or Calvados

1 cup orange juice

Ice cubes

1 pint Normandy cider (see page 74)

1 pint sparkling water or Ginger Beer (see page 58)

Put the sliced fruit in the jug, add the Pommeau or Calvados and orange juice, and leave to steep until guests arrive. Half-fill the jug with ice cubes and top up with the cider and sparkling water or Ginger Beer.

Stir and serve in tall glasses or tumblers.

New Hampshire cider sangria

Serves 4 to 8

1 orange

1 lime

1 lemon

1/4 to 1/2 cup sherry or Spanish brandy

Ice cubes

1 quart Three Counties Cider (see page 76) or 1/2 cider, 1/2 Sparkling Lemonade (see page 50)

Freshly grated nutmeg

Superfine sugar, for extra sweetness, if necessary

You will also need

Wide-necked carafe or jug

Nutmeg grater

Spirit measure

Steve Wood at Farnum Hill Cider in New Hampshire says that if you're looking for a craft-made, fruit-flavored cider you won't find one, but suggests making your own by simply pouring a light, summery hard cider over peach slices or raspberries, or even use it to make sangria. If you prefer a sweet drink, use sweet cider; if you prefer a drier style choose dry cider.

Slice the fruit and put it in the jug, add the measured sherry or brandy and leave to steep until guests arrive. Half-fill the jug with ice cubes and top up with Three Counties Cider, or 1/2 cider/1/2 Sparkling Lemonade. Add a grating of nutmeg, stir, and taste, and if necessary stir in some superfine sugar. Serve in wine glasses.

Poverty Lane Orchard Pimm's

Makes 1 large glass

Ice

1 part Pimm's No 1

2 parts Three Counties Cider (see page 76)

2 parts Sparkling Lemonade (see page 50)

1 tbsp Florida Cocktail Cordial (see page 16), optional

Slice of apple

Slice of orange

Slice of cucumber

Slice of borage or mint

You will also need

Spirit measure

Swizzle sticks

Here is another of Steve Wood's creative ways of serving cider, but this time it's a slant on a classic British summer drink. I think it should come with a health warning, though, given that both cider and Pimm's are drinks that slip down very easily on a hot summer day; put them together in the same glass and add lots of pretty fruit and ice and you could be in trouble... in the nicest possible way. You can leave out the Pimm's to make a lighter, fruitier drink.

Half-fill the glass with ice and add the Pimm's, Three Counties Cider, Sparkling Lemonade, and Florida Cocktail Cordial. Swizzle, then add the fruit, cucumber and borage or mint. Swizzle again and serve in a large glass.

Rosemary & thyme perry infusion

Fruit and flavored ciders and perries are popular drinks in the UK, Europe, and Scandinavia but they can be made much more successfully at home simply by crushing berries and other fruit and topping them up with cider to create fresh, fruity fragrance in the cider without the need for additives. I recommend that you try this unusual perry and herb infusion.

Serves 2 to 4

2 sprigs of rosemary

2 sprigs of thyme

1 1/2 pints perry (see pages 76 and 80)

2 tbsp sugar syrup (see page 108), optional

You will also need

Jug and large glasses

Put the herbs in a jug and bash lightly with the end of a rolling pin. Add the perry and sugar syrup (if using). Pour into glasses and serve.

Note: Much traditional perry and cider is still rather than sparkling and the connoisseur would rather drink them at room temperature than on ice. I have therefore not specified still or sparkling, nor included ice in this recipe. I will leave these choices up to you.

Charlotte rose

This pretty punch is made with Rose Petal Cordial, Strawberry Rum Cordial, and Cointreau or Orangello (the orange version of Limoncello) liqueurs and wine or cider. Experiment with other cordials, but stick with pink or red ones to retain the lovely color.

Serves 8 to 12

Iceberg (see box, page 161)

1/2 cup Cointreau or Orangello (see page 120)

1/2 cup Strawberry Rum Cordial (see page 136)

1/2 cup Rose Petal Cordial (see page 29)

1 to 2 small oranges, sliced

9 oz strawberries, cut in half

Juice and thinly peeled zest of 4 small oranges

1 1/2 quarts white wine or hard cider, chilled

Shake of Angostura bitters

Superfine sugar, to taste

1 strawberry for each glass, to serve

You will also need

1 quart (32 fl oz) plastic tub with lid

Spirit measure

Punchbowl and cups or glasses

The day before the Charlotte Rose is required, make an iceberg by filling a quart-sized plastic tub with water (leaving a small space for expansion), seal it with a lid, and put it in the freezer.

An hour before your guests arrive, put the measured liqueurs, cordial, fruit, thinly peeled zest, and fruit juices in a punchbowl and leave to steep. When your first guests arrive, add the iceberg, the chilled wine or cider and the bitters, and stir. Taste and add sugar if required. Put a strawberry in each glass and serve.

Illustrated on page 146

Left Artisan Black Velvet (left) and Lemonade, Lime & Light Ale Shandy

Artisan black velvet

I learned to love Guinness as a nursing mother (back in the day when stout or Guinness was "prescribed" by midwives to new mothers.) Since then it has become my preferred winter thirst-quencher and pick-me-up. When it comes to party time, the addition of homemade Fennel Flower "Prosecco" transforms it into a light, frothy, sweet-and-sour delight. Use regular Champagne or Prosecco if you don't have anything homemade. If you love Guinness, you will love this.

Makes 1 glass

1/2 cup chilled Guinness

1/2 cup chilled Fennel Flower "Prosecco" (see page 48)

You will also need

Stemmed glass or cup

Carefully pour the Guinness into the glass, then top up with Fennel Flower "Prosecco".

Lemonade, lime & light ale shandy

Shandies have been popular alcoholic summer thirst-quenchers in Northern Europe for decades. Then suddenly, in 2012, brewers around the world became obsessed with beer and lemon or lemonade blends, exalting shandy's status from run-of-the-mill to top-notch. You can make your own shandy at home simply by mixing beer and homemade Sparkling Lemonade and adding lime or lemon juice. Or if you like a drier style, try it with the Lemon Sherbet recipe in this book.

Serves 2

2 tbsp + 2 tsp Ginger Cordial (see page 21)

1 pint chilled Lemon Sherbet or Sparkling Lemonade (see pages 22, 50)

1 pint chilled light ale

Juice of 1 lime

Pinch of mixed spice, optional

2 lime wedges

You will also need

2 x 1 pint (16 fl oz) glasses

Divide the Ginger Cordial between the 2 glasses. Pour half the Lemon Sherbet or Sparkling Lemonade into each glass, then top with the light ale and half the lime juice per glass. Add a pinch of spice if preferred. Swirl and serve with a lime wedge.

"Wassail"—Christmas spiced ale

Wassail, from Middle English *wæs hæl*, means "good health." So here's a hearty festive drink to welcome in the season. If you don't have a punchbowl and ladle, improvise with the largest vessel you can find, and if it isn't an elegant affair simply wrap it in a white linen cloth or pretty tablecloth, decorate it with ivy and ribbons to give it a party feel, and serve the spiced ale with a small jug. This is a dry drink that works well with Guinness or stout as well as ale.

Serves 8 to 12

Handful of white raisins

5 fl oz Marsala, sherry, brandy or rum

1/2 cup Ginger Cordial (see page 21) or 2/3 cup superfine sugar

Pinch of grated nutmeg, ginger and cinnamon

2 quarts ale, porter, stout or other dark ale

Ice, optional

You will also need

Punchbowl and cups or glasses

Put the white raisins in the punchbowl, add the measured Marsala, sherry or brandy, Ginger Cordial or sugar, and the spices. Leave to steep. When your guests arrive, add ice (if preferred) and the ale. Stir and serve in cups.

Happy hours

Artisan cocktails & elegant mocktails

Artisan cocktails

I was a child of the 1950s and my mother drank something called "Gin & It," made from gin and sweet vermouth, with an all-important maraschino cherry on a cocktail stick. I can smell and see it now; she drank it in a glass etched with a spider's web with the bright-red cherry sitting broodingly at the bottom in its dark, rich, sweet pond.

These were the days when men still donned white tie and tails at dances and women wore Chanel-style dresses with big skirts and long gloves. Smoking was a trouble-free, innocent pursuit, and both my parents carried cigarette cases. On special occasions my mother filled her's with Sobranies: dazzling chalk-colored, gold-tipped cigarettes instead of the usual white ones.

All this was before Mr Schweppes burst onto the scene with his little mixer bottles of bitter lemon, orange, tonic, and soda, revolutionizing the drinks arena—in our house, at least. After that, cocktail bars became old hat and disappeared, or they became confined to internationally renowned hotels, where low-key yet incredibly smooth bartenders plied the art of the cocktail.

I worked in Rome in the seventies, near the top of the Spanish Steps, around the corner from the Hassler Roma hotel. There, *il barista* taught me to appreciate the finer points of a Whiskey Sour: shaken, not stirred. Meanwhile, on trips back to London the bartender at The Dorchester's cocktail bar made an equally delicious Whiskey Sour, but his was stirred, not shaken.

These days the cocktail is no longer confined to hallowed halls. Cocktail bars have sprung up in cities the world over. Whether in New York, Paris, Chicago, or Berlin, the choice of venues is endless, but you still can't beat those classic bars that have been making cocktails since before the Roaring Twenties.

The kit

An elegant cocktail shaker and glasses are essential to set the scene. Fine linen napkins, coasters, and vintage trays add drama. An assortment of swizzle sticks, stirrers, cocktail sticks, and the like adds razzamatazz. A citrus-juice squeezer and a spirit measure are useful. The rest is down to you.

A standard measure of spirit for a cocktail is 2 shots (2 fl oz or 1/4 cup). You can buy a tiny measuring cup called a jigger made especially for the job; it's often attached, base to base, to a half measuring cup.

The artisan cocktail Most of the cocktails in this book are based on classics but have an artisan twist to the ingredients and their names. A Mojito made with Syrop de Menthe becomes Le Mojito (page 166). The Pink Elephant becomes "bejewelled" because it has pomegranate seeds (the "jewels") in it (page 162). Some are my own inventions to honor citizens of our time, such as Mr President, an elegant blend of homemade Coffee Cream Liqueur and cola, and The Duke of Cambridge, a smooth yet gentle mix of orange juice, egg, and Vanilla Brandy (page 168).

Short or long? Personally speaking, I love a short cocktail in a martini glass! It is the glass that makes the cocktail, and anything that comes in a highball or tumbler to my mind does not merit the title "cocktail." Instead, it is a drink or an aperitif. But that is just my opinion—the rest of the world thinks differently and so this chapter contains both short and long cocktails.

If you prefer a long drink, all short cocktails can be served in big glasses. Simply partially fill the glass with crushed ice, pour the original cocktail over the top, and add soda, sparkling water, or lemonade. Conversely, long cocktails can be served short by shaking the basic ingredients with ice rather than putting ice in the glass, and reducing the amount of mixer.

Nearly all the cocktail and mocktail recipes in this chapter are for one, except those for a couple of nonalcoholic punches. If you are making more, simply increase the quantities in the correct proportion. It is possible to make up to six short cocktails at a time in a shaker, but make sure there is room for plenty of ice. A short cocktail *must* be served ice cold.

"Shaken, not stirred" Some cocktails should be shaken and some stirred. If shaking is for you, half-fill

Make an "iceberg"

For chilling punches, make an 'iceberg'. When you are making cocktails on this scale, ice cubes simply melt too quickly, making the drink watery. Instead, almost fill two 1 quart plastic containers with water, but make sure you leave enough room for expansion during freezing. Put the lid on tightly and place in the freezer. When solid, turn the ice blocks out into a plastic bag and store until required.

your shaker with ice, add your ingredients, and with as much show as you can muster, give it all you have got—a short shake just will not do! Think bartender in *Cocktail*. However, it's not all for show. It's also about the taste and temperature of what ends up in the glass.

Ice Ice for cocktails should be fresh from the freezer, not half-melted. Long cocktails are best shaken with ice and then the cocktail poured into the glass with the ice. Short cocktails are best shaken with a few ice cubes, then strained into the glass. Most cocktail shakers have a strainer inside the lid and then a top that fits over that.

Talking of the top, don't forget to put it back on before you shake—it's easy to forget!

If you don't have an ice maker, always have a big bag or two of ice handy before you start—the average household ice tray is just not going to provide enough.

To make crushed ice, put a mound of ice cubes in the middle of a clean cloth, tie the four corners of the cloth together, and smash the cloth a few times against a solid surface.

Just for the record Cocktails are strong drinks and should be sipped slowly. I recently found myself in a cocktail bar knowing I had to drive home. I asked the bartender which cocktail I could drink and still be within the legal limit. He replied "None! Have a glass of Champagne instead!"

The alternative, of course, would be to consider a nonalcoholic cocktail, such as those described from page 170 onwards.

Right: Bejewelled Pink Elephant, see page 162

Bejewelled Pink Elephant

The Pink Elephant is a classic cocktail with a bourbon base. Like so many classics there are many variations. I have added homemade pomegranate cordial and pomegranate seeds—the "jewels"—to the glass, thus creating the "bejewelled" elephant.

Makes 1 glass

1 tsp pomegranate jewels (seeds)

2 2/3 shots (2 3/4 fl oz) Bourbon Shrub (page 118), or 2 shots (2 fl oz) bourbon + 2/3 shot (4 tsp) lemon juice

2 tsp Syrop de Grenadine (page 20)

1 tbsp egg white (see box, page 165)

You will also need

Ice

Classic coupette, martini, or similar glass

Cocktail shaker & strainer

Put a teaspoon of pomegranate seeds in the bottom of your glass. Pour the bourbon and Syrop de Grenadine in a shaker and add the egg white. Shake well, half-fill with ice and shake again. Strain into the glass and serve.

Illustrated on page 161

Peach Vodka Bellini

This take on the classic Venetian aperitif has an added artisan bouquet from the Peach & Vanilla Vodka and a touch of Rose Petal Cordial. I drank my first Bellini cocktail years ago, on the terrace of the romantic Hotel Villa Cipriani in Asolo, in the hills near Venice.

Makes 1 glass

2 shots (2 fl oz) iced Peach & Vanilla Vodka (page 135)

1/2 cup (4 fl oz) chilled Prosecco

Dash of Rose Petal Cordial (page 29)

To serve

Sliver of peach or a rose petal

You will also need

Champagne flute or cup

Put the Peach & Vanilla Vodka in the freezer and the Prosecco in the refrigerator for an hour or so before making. Put a dash of Rose Petal Cordial in the flute, add the vodka, carefully fill the glass with Prosecco, swirl, and serve with a sliver of peach or topped with a rose petal.

Variation: Use Fennel Flower "Prosecco" or Elderflower "Champagne" (pages 48, 49) instead of the Prosecco.

Cherry Brandy Country Cocktail

This cocktail is a variation on a classic Champagne Cocktail.

Makes 1 glass

1 shot (1 fl oz) chilled Cherry Brandy (page 127)

1 cup + 2 tbsp (5 fl oz) chilled Fennel Flower "Prosecco" or Elderflower "Champagne"(pages 48, 49)

To serve

Maraschino cherry

You will also need

Champagne cup or flute and cocktail stick

Put the Cherry Brandy and "Prosecco" in the refrigerator for an hour or so before making. When ready to serve, pour the iced Cherry Brandy into the glass and top up with chilled Fennel Flower "Prosecco" or Elderflower "Champagne," add a maraschino cherry on a cocktail stick, and serve.

Variation: Try with regular Champagne, sparkling wine, or Prosecco.

Opposite: Peach Vodka Bellini (back) and Cherry Brandy Country Cocktail

Opposite: Whiskey Sour Amalfitana

Whiskey Sour Amalfitana

This is a variation on one of my all-time favorite cocktails, the whiskey sour, normally made with whiskey and lemon juice. I have used my homemade Limoncello San Vigilio alongside the Scotch whiskey and coined the name "Whiskey Sour Amalfitana" in honor of the stunning Amalfi coast in Italy, where lemon trees abound and Limoncello is a local specialty.
I have given two versions here: one to make in a shaker with egg white and the other in a glass without. Both are delicious—so the choice is up to you.

Makes 1 glass

1 shot (1 fl oz) Scotch whiskey

1 shot (1 fl oz) Limoncello San Vigilio (page 120)

1 shot (1 fl oz) lemon juice

2 drops of Angostura bitters

1 tsp of sugar syrup (see box, below)

To serve

Twist of lemon

You will also need

Ice

Highball glass or similar and swizzle stick

Part-fill the glass with ice, add all the ingredients, and swizzle. Serve with a twist of lemon.

Whiskey Sour Amalfitana: the other way

Makes 1 glass

1 shot (1 fl oz) Scotch whiskey

1 shot (1 fl oz) Limoncello San Vigilio (page 120)

1 shot (1 fl oz) lemon juice

2 drops of Angostura bitters

1 tsp sifted confectioners' sugar or sugar syrup

1 tbsp egg white

To serve

Twist of lemon

You will also need

Ice

Cocktail shaker & strainer

Highball glass or similar

Put the whiskey, Limoncello, lemon juice, bitters, and sugar into a shaker. Add the egg white and shake well. Half-fill the shaker with ice and shake again. Strain into a highball glass and serve with a twist of lemon.

Special ingredients

Many cocktails contain egg white, which, when shaken vigorously with the other ingredients, will add a frothy white head to the cocktail. It is important to do this before adding ice, because the extreme cold inhibits the build-up of froth—so much so, that eggs destined for this purpose should be at room temperature, and not straight from the refrigerator.

Sweetness is, as you would expect, an important characteristic of many cocktails. Depending on the characteristics of the cider, wine, beer, or ginger beer you choose, the amount of sweetening you need to add will vary. Add a teaspoon of sifted confectioners' sugar to the shaker and shake again if you feel the cocktail is too dry. If making the cocktail in a glass, add a little sugar syrup.

To make sugar syrup, gently boil equal quantities of sugar and water to dissolve the sugar, let it cool, transfer to a bottle, then store in the refrigerator.

Le Mojito

This is a classic Mojito, with all those bittersweet citrus notes rounded off with mint syrup, as well as the classic mint leaves.

Serve short or long. Makes 1 glass

2 shots (2 fl oz) white rum

Juice of ½ lime

⅔ shot (4 tsp) Syrop de Menthe (page 34)

10 mint leaves

Dash of Angostura bitters

Top up as necessary with soda

To serve

Sprig of mint or a twist of lime zest

You will also need

Ice

Cocktail shaker & strainer

Coupette, martini, or similar glass

Half-fill a cocktail shaker with ice, add the rum, lime juice, Syrop de Menthe, mint leaves, and a dash of bitters. Seal the cocktail shaker and shake well. Strain into a coupette, martini, or similar glass and top with a small sprig of mint or a twist of lime zest.

If you prefer a long drink, pour Le Mojito into a tumbler and add ice, soda or sparkling water.

Variation: For a Still Waters Mojito, use one of the many fruit cordials in the "Still Waters Run Deep" chapter instead of the Syrop de Menthe and 10 mint leaves to create new and colorful Mojitos instantly. Embellish the glass with fruit to suit.

Damson Gin Fizz

Yet another take here on a classic cocktail, the gin fizz, and what better variation than a damson one? Add an extra shot of gin to give more depth of flavor to the cocktail.

Makes 1 glass

2 shots (2 fl oz) Damson Gin (page 138)

1 shot (1 fl oz) gin, optional

1/3 shot (2 tsp) lemon juice

1 tbsp egg white

Soda or sparkling water to top up

To serve

Slice of lemon

You will also need

Ice

Cocktail shaker & strainer

Highball glass or similar

Swizzle stick

Put the Damson Gin and the single shot of gin (if using) in the cocktail shaker with the lemon juice and egg white. Shake hard to combine all the ingredients and to make the egg froth. Add a handful of ice to the shaker and a few cubes into a highball glass. Shake again, pour into the glass, add a slice of lemon, and top up with soda.

The Duke of Cambridge

I created this cocktail on the day Prince George (third in line to the British throne) was born. Vanilla, brandy, orange juice, and egg seemed like a good mix for congratulating his father.

Makes 1 glass

2 shots (2 fl oz) Vanilla Brandy (page 140)

1/2 cup (4 fl oz) freshly squeezed orange juice

1 small organic egg

Ice and slice of orange to garnish

You will also need

Coupette, martini, or similar glass

Cocktail shaker & strainer

Put all the ingredients in the cocktail shaker, shake well to combine, then add plenty of ice and shake again. Strain into a coupette, martini, or similar glass, top with a slice of orange, and serve at once.

Jumping Jack Flash

Make this with chilled fresh apple juice and it's a liquid dessert. Add hard cider and it becomes a rollercoaster of flavors. For the best results use fresh home- or farm-made, single-apple-variety juice rather than ones made from concentrate. Frost the glass before you start.

Makes 1 glass

1 small peeled lump of ginger root

1 small piece of stem ginger

1 to 2 tbsp sifted confectioners' sugar

2 shots (2 fl oz) Spiced Walnut & Chocolate Cream Liqueur (page 124)

1 shot (1 fl oz) chilled fresh sweet apple juice

1 shot (1 fl oz) hard cider

Ice

You will also need

Classic coupette, martini or similar glass

Cocktail shaker & strainer

Spread the confectioners' sugar on a plate. Bash the ginger root and rub the rim of the glass with it. Invert the glass and dip it in the confectioners' sugar. Turn the glass back up and leave to dry. When ready to serve, add the stem ginger to the glass. Half-fill a cocktail shaker with ice, add the Spiced Walnut & Chocolate Liqueur, apple juice, and cider, and shake well. Strain into the glass, being careful not to splash the frosting.

Variation: For a sweeter, less dynamic drink, use all apple juice instead of a mixture of juice and cider.

Mr President

Elegant cocktails need names, and because this one contains the quintessentially American cola and I'm a fan of Mr Obama, I have named it after him. Do you think he will mind?

Makes 1 glass

2 shots (2 fl oz) Coffee Cream Liqueur (page 144)

1 shot (1 fl oz) dark rum

Cola to top up, as desired

Crushed ice

You will also need

1 tumbler or similar

1 swizzle stick

Fill the glass 2/3 full with ice. Pour over the Coffee Cream Liqueur and the dark rum and top up with the cola. Swizzle and enjoy.

Opposite from left: The Duke of Cambridge, Jumping Jack Flash and Mr President

A twist in the tail: mocktails

Just because we're not drinking alcohol at a party or celebration does not mean that we don't want a beautiful and elegant drink. Therefore I have created a selection of nonalcoholic cocktails to set the taste buds and senses reeling, using some of the soft drinks featured in this book. Some of my mocktails have adult appeal, while others are distinctly child-friendly.

Prohibition and Tropical Storm are short cocktails served in the classic "must-have" coupette or martini glass (page 172). These drinks pack such a punch that it is difficult to believe they are alcohol-free. There are also pretty and refreshing party punches such as the sweet and mellow Pussyfoot and the vibrant Heatwave (page 178).

For something simpler and thirst-quenching, look towards Beach Blanket and Flirty, two cordial-based drinks: one sweet and one dry (page 176).

For me, the glass is of huge importance. If everyone is drinking Champagne from a flute with a strawberry on the side, I want my sparkling water laced with elderflower cordial served the same way. The eye plays such a big role in the enjoyment of what we eat and drink, and how my aperitif is served is the benchmark of my whole experience.

Garden Path: lavender ice cream soda

If you love lavender-flavored cookies and cakes, you are going to adore this pleasing lavender drink-cum-ice cream.

Makes 1 glass

2 to 3 scoops of vanilla ice cream

6 to 8 ice cubes

1 cup Lavender Spritz (page 56)

To serve

1 sprig of lavender

You will also need

1 sundae glass

1 long spoon

Alternate scoops of ice cream with a few ice cubes in the glass, finishing with ice cream. Top up with Lavender Spritz. Stir and serve with a sprig of lavender.

Variation: If lavender isn't your thing, make an ice cream soda with one of the many fruit cordials listed in the book, such as Spiced Blackberry Tonic (page 36) or blackberry or raspberry cordial (Variation, page 26) with soda or sparkling water. For something with more panache, try adding Ginger Cordial instead (page 21). If you crave something sweeter, add Sparkling Lemonade (page 50). To vary the flavors, top up with other carbonated drinks (see "Family Fizz," page 44).

Prohibition

This is another of my own inventions: a riot of flavors in a glass that makes an exciting, nonalcoholic drink using fresh apple juice, also called Prohibition Cider.

Makes 1 glass

1 cup + 2 tbsp sweet farm-bottled or your own homemade Carey Apple Juice (page 40)

1 shot (1 fl oz) chilled Syrop de Menthe Extra (page 34)

1 tbsp egg white

To serve

2 chocolate sticks and dark chocolate, to grate

You will also need

4 ice cubes

Coupette, martini, or similar glass

Cocktail shaker

Put the apple juice, Syrop de Menthe Extra, and egg white in the cocktail shaker and shake well. Put a handful of ice in the shaker and shake again. Pour the frothy apple juice into the glass, taking care to top the glass with the froth. Add a grating of dark chocolate and 2 chocolate sticks and serve.

Variation: Use Spiced Blackberry Tonic (page 36) instead of Syrop de Menthe.

Tropical Storm

This is a pretty mocktail, to be served in a coupette or martini glass. Vary the fruits to make new flavors. Taste before serving since the sweetness of the pineapple can vary and this will change the dynamic of the drink. Add extra Ginger Cordial for extra depth of flavor.

Makes 1 glass

½ cup crushed pineapple + juice or pineapple juice

1 shot (1 fl oz) Ginger Cordial (page 21)

1 tbsp egg white

1 small piece stem ginger

Sparkling water, as desired

You will also need

4 ice cubes

Blender, if the pineapple is not already crushed

Coupette, martini, or similar glass

Cocktail shaker

Small, pretty spoon

If using canned, sliced pinapple, put it in a blender with the juice and blitz for 30 seconds, or until crushed. When using unsweetened or fresh pineapple it may be necessary to add an extra teaspoon of sugar syrup (see box, page 165) or confectioners' sugar.

Put the pineapple, Ginger Cordial, and the egg white in a cocktail shaker and shake hard to mix the ingredients well. Add the ice cubes and shake again. Put the stem ginger in the glass with the spoon.

Pour in the cocktail, top up with a little sparkling water if required, stir, and serve.

Variation: If you prefer a long drink, put the cocktail in a tall glass and top up with Sparkling Lemonade (page 50). Make a Summer Shower by using crushed strawberries or raspberries and Florida Cocktail Cordial (page 16) instead of the pineapple and Ginger Cordial.

Heatwave

This drink has such a variety of flavors that it's hard to believe it is nonalcoholic. If you don't have lemongrass, add the freshly pared zest of the limes.

Serves 4

½ cup Ginger Cordial (page 21)

Juice of 2 limes

1 ½ pints Ginger Beer (page 58)

1 stem of lemon grass or finely peeled lime zest

To serve

1 extra stem of lemongrass, slit into quarters lengthways to use as swizzle sticks

You will also need

Ice

Large jug and 4 tall glasses

Put the Ginger Cordial in the jug with the juice of the limes. Half-fill with ice and top up with Ginger Beer. Lightly bash the lemongrass with a hammer or rolling pin, and use it to stir the drink. Pour into 4 glasses and serve each with a lemongrass swizzle stick.

Pussyfoot

The first time I saw a Pussyfoot cocktail I was on a family vacation. Once a week the hotel held a children's party in the ballroom before dinner. I was given a glass containing a rich, red potion swathed in fruit and I was too scared to drink it. It looked more like an adult cocktail than the usual watery orangeade we childen were treated to. I wasn't very old, and to this day I remember the waiter trying his best to reassure me it was alright to drink.

Serves 8

Iceberg (see box, page 161)

½ cup + 2 tbsp Syrop de Grenadine (page 20), raspberry or strawberry cordial (Variation, page 26)

Juice of 4 large oranges

Juice and finely pared zest of 2 lemons

Angostura bitters

2 oranges, sliced

2 lemons, sliced

Seeds from a pomegranate

Ginger Beer or Sparkling Lemonade (pages 58, 50) to top up

To serve

8 maraschino cherries

You will also need

Punchbowl

Punch cups or glasses

The day before the Pussyfoot punch is required, make an iceberg as directed on page 161. An hour before your guests arrive, put the Syrop de Grenadine, fruit juices, zest, and bitters in a punchbowl. Add the sliced citrus fruit and the pomegranate seeds and leave to macerate. When your first guests arrive, add the iceberg and the Ginger Beer or Sparkling Lemonade and stir. Put a cherry in each glass and serve.

Oasis of calm

Teas, tisanes & spicy brews

Teas, tisanes & spicy brews

Don't just reach for a tea-bag carton the next time you need a reviving hot drink. Flowers, herbs, and seeds gathered in your garden, backyard, or out on a ramble in the country make refreshing tisanes, teas, and infusions. The spice cupboard, too, holds the key to a wealth of rich, warming drinks with coffee and chocolate bases.

This chapter is split into sections featuring herbal infusions with mint, thyme, sweet cicely, rosemary, and fennel; flower teas with jasmine and lime; rosehip and citrus drinks and spiced brews with cardamom and nutmeg. Most important is the special pleasure gained in creating your own drinks.

Taste Taste is everything when it comes to hot drinks; I like my coffee short, strong, and black but I drink very weak tea. Experiment and vary quantities to suit yourself. I don't add sugar to hot drinks, but sugar does enhance flavor and you may prefer to use it.

One for the pot There is nothing like tea that has been correctly made and brewed in a pot. Tea bags and infusors have their place, but the pot gives the leaves, flowers, seeds, and spices the space they need to brew and allow their flavors to develop. Whatever the hot drink you are making, always heat the pot first (see box, opposite page).

Drying herbs

- Wait for the herbs to come into flower.
- Pick the herbs or seed heads on a dry, sunny morning.
- Tie them in bunches with raffia or fine string.
- Hang them upside-down, using butcher's hooks or clothespins, in a dry, airy spot away from the sun to ensure they keep their color. The frame of an indoor clothesline is good.
- Leave the bunches until completely dry.
- Transfer to a plastic bag and tie loosely, making sure there is no air in the bag.
- Using your hands or a rolling pin, crush the leaves or seed heads.
- Discard the stems and store the leaves or seeds in a tea canister or jar in the dark.
- Do not store dried herbs for more than a year; the herbs will taste dusty and spoil the tisane's flavor.

Moroccan fresh mint tea

Makes a pot for 4 to 6

4 heaped tsp Moroccan tea

1 bunch fresh mint, washed and wrung dry

Boiling water

You will also need

4 tsp sugar, optional

Tea strainer

For me, mint tea is synonymous with Morocco: a symbol of welcome and hospitality wherever you go. It is very sweet, very strong, and revitalizing. Traditionally tea and mint should be boiled together, but simply brewing them together in a pot makes a refreshing everyday pick-me-up.

Warm the teapot. Put the Moroccan tea in the heated teapot, add the mint, and pour the boiling water over the top. Let stand for 10 minutes, then add the sugar (if using) and stir well. Pour the hot tea through a tea strainer into cups. Alternatively, strain into a jug, leave to cool, and serve on ice.

Variation: For a refreshing sparkling summer drink, add extra sugar to taste and when cold stir in ½ cup lemon juice and top up with 1½ cups sparkling water.

Warming the pot

Whatever hot drink you're making, always heat the pot first by rinsing it out with a little boiling water before adding the dry ingredients. This will help encourage a good brew.

Tisanes

On a recent trip to France, a friend and I spotted cars parked on some on the roadside in the middle of nowhere and noticed people hovering in the bushes. They were picking something, but what?

We wondered about wild asparagus but it was too early. It was March, so they were certainly not mushroom hunters. We wandered around but could not find anything in particular; there was an odd clump of flowering wild thyme but nothing else.

When we finally honed our French enough to shape a conversation we approached a couple who were busily stuffing plastic supermarket bags with the thyme. They explained with great enthusiasm that they were gathering the thyme to make tisanes because it was in flower: the optimum time. They were so excited about it. Of course, this makes perfect sense because herbs are at their most aromatic when in flower.

The French, of course, are devotees of the tisane. Back in the sixties, when no one outside of France contemplated drinking herbal teas other than the odd eccentric, my best friend in London, who was French, used to offer *une petite tisane*. Whatever her mood, whatever the moment, whatever the problem, be it mental or physical, a little tisane seemed to solve everything.

I later went to live in Italy, where chamomile is a cure-all for most things: the answer to stress, indigestion, insomnia. I later discovered in the Far East that root ginger peelings make comforting, warming tea—great for settling the stomach.

You can use fresh or dried herbs to make tisanes. Fresh herbs make delicate infusions and therefore require a good handful of sprigs to make a pot, while dried herbs give a much more intense flavor and need to be used sparingly. While flower infusions work best with light teas (see pages 186 to 187), it's best to combine fresh herbs with strong teas, eg. Moroccan Mint Tea (page 182), or simply to infuse fresh or dried herbs by themselves to create more delicate brews.

Blending Try blending tisanes with herbs, leaves, and flowers to make lingering and evocative flavors. Also remember the healing and aromatic leaves, such as nettle, hawthorn and raspberry. If delicate herbal brews are not for you, try mixing classic tea leaves and blends from some of the vibrant young companies that seem to be springing up everywhere, or the established emporiums (eg. Celestial Seasonings) with fresh herbs and spices. This brings delicate fragrance to established flavors. Although it is possible to buy a huge array of wonderful artisan herb and spiced brews, there is always a place for making your own.

Herb garden tisanes

Makes a pot of tea for 4

With fresh herbs

4 large sprigs of thyme, sweet cicely, and borage

2 small sprigs of rosemary and borage or herbs of choice

Boiling water

With dried herbs

3 level tsp of mixed freshly dried herbs, such as thyme and rosemary, mixed with 1/2 tsp of fennel and 1/2 tsp sweet cicely seeds

Boiling water

You will also need

Tea strainer

Herb teas are simple to make and can be made in several ways. Remember that fresh herbs are delicate, but drying intensifies the flavor, so use less when making tea with dried herbs. Plants such as dill and fennel produce seeds that make good, if pungent, herbal tea.

Warm the teapot. Add all the fresh herb stems or the dried herbs and seeds to the heated teapot, add boiling water, and leave to steep for 5 to 10 minutes. Strain the hot tea into cups and enjoy.

Drying flowers & leaves

Whether drying flowers for tea or other purposes, the method is the same. Include marigold petals to make exotic jasmine flowers go further, or dry rose petals or lavender as an alternative to jasmine.

- If you're going to make tea with flowers and leaves, you must be sure that the plants they come from have not been sprayed with any chemicals.
- Gather flowers and leaves in warm, dry weather, not after rain or watering—they *must* be dry.
- Jasmine flowers can be picked up from the ground but only those that are freshly fallen and still white. Rose petals can be gathered just before they fall—as the rose is "going over" (this saves a lot of picking up from the ground).
- Gather flowers daily.
- Spread a folded clean, dry dishcloth on a large tray.
- Spread the flowers or leaves out on the cloth in a single layer with plenty of space around it.
- Put the tray in a warm, dry, dark place; make sure there is plenty of space around it for air to circulate.
- Leave for a few days. When completely dry, transfer the flowers, petals, or leaves to an airtight tea canister or glass jar and keep in the dark until required.
- Enjoy the scent when you open the jar to make the tea.

Jasmine flower & green tea

We tend to think of jasmine tea as being exotic; its sweet, heavy fragrance wakens memories of faraway cities, warm nights, and clusters of waxy white flowers and abundant fresh, green foliage spilling over garden walls, offering just a hint of the secrets within. Jasmine actually grows well in more temperate climes, where it likes a warm, sheltered, sunny spot on a wall. You don't need to add many flowers to green tea leaves because their role is simply to add a light perfume to the brew. Alternatively, you can add a handful of jasmine flowers to your tea canister and shake to distribute them among the tea leaves. Try adding a few jasmine flowers to drinking water, which creates a similar perfumed effect if left overnight.

Makes a pot for 2

- 2 heaped tsp green tea
- 6 dried jasmine flowers or scented rose petals, lavender, or marigold petals
- Boiling water

You will also need

- Oriental teapot
- Small cups
- Tea strainer

Warm the teapot. Put the tea in the teapot, add the flowers, and pour the boiling water over the top. Let stand for 2 minutes; stir well. Pour the hot tea through a tea strainer into the cups and serve at once.

Note: Sweet flowers and petals such as lavender and rose can be quite sickly on their own and not to everyone's taste. Adding them to green tea creates a more subtle infusion with more depth of flavor, and provides all the benefits of green tea, plus the flowers.

Lime & other flower infusions

Avenues of lime trees line many city streets and parks. They grow into magnificent leafy trees, but it's in June when they come into flower that they come into their own. The small not very flower-like blossom gives off an elusive heady fragrance that is associated more readily with expensive perfumes and glamorous women than parks and city streets. So I wasn't surprised to learn that in folklore, limes are widely considered a female tree and have links to fertility. Once you've discovered the lime tree's secret, you will make sure that you pass their way when they are in flower just to bathe in their glorious perfume. One way of capturing the scent is to pick the flowers and dry them (see box, opposite), then keep them in an airtight tea canister or jar, store in the dark, and use them to make infusions.

Makes a pot of tea for 1 or 1 large mug

- 1 tbsp lime flowers
- Boiling water

You will also need

- Small teapot or large mug
- Infuser bag

Fill the infuser bag with flowers and put in the heated teapot or mug. Add the boiling water and let steep for 5 to 10 minutes. Sip this refreshing tea, breathe in the sweet scent, and enjoy the moment.

Variation: Infuse other flowers in the same way: eg. rose petals, jasmine, orange, elderflowers and hibiscus. But use lavender sparingly: 1 tsp per pot is enough.

Following pages: Lime Flower Infusion (left) and Jasmine Flower & Green Tea

Rosehip tea

Rosehips are found growing wild all over the place and are full of vitamin C. Our grandmothers encouraged daily doses, and modern science has dubbed them a superfood. Often prescribed as syrup, the benefits of rosehips can be imbibed in tea form, thus avoiding high intake of sugar. This tea is so dazzlingly fragrant that it puts the actual flavor in the shade. However, the delicately sweet and evocative taste of roses remains on the palate long after the tea has gone. Teas made with rosehips need brewing for at least 10 minutes; it is therefore advisable to use a pot.

Makes a small pot for 2

1 heaped tbsp dried rosehips, crushed

Boiling water

You will also need

Glass infuser or teapot

Tea strainer (if using a teapot)

Put the crushed rosehips and seeds in the heated infuser or pot, add the boiling water, and leave to steep for 10 minutes. Pour and enjoy.

Variation: Try using a small handful of the dried peel of tangerines, oranges, limes, and lemons (see box, below) to make alternative fragrant citrus teas using the same method as rosehip tea.

Note: Whatever you do, don't drink hot, simply strain and drink iced or reheated later on.

Drying rosehips & citrus zest

- Using a potato peeler, finely shave the rind from oranges, lemons, limes, and grapefruit; peel tangerines, clementines, etc.
- Spread the citrus zest or rosehips out on a baking or cookie sheet and leave in a low oven at 100 to 125°F overnight, or until rock-hard.
- Leave to cool.
- Crush the rosehips but leave citrus zest and peel whole.
- The hips and zest will keep their fragrance for 12 months if stored in a tea canister or jar in the dark.
- Thin slices of lemon, lime and orange can be dried on trays lined with parchment paper in the same way overnight in the oven. These can be used as decorations to float on herbal teas.

Ginger root & lemongrass tea

I always make myself ginger tea when I'm preparing root ginger for a recipe. All you need to do is collect the ginger peelings, put them in an infuser in a mug, and top up with boiling water. You can, of course, make a more elegant pot by following this recipe using ginger only. Ginger tea is delicious, warming, and excellent for settling upset stomachs or indigestion, so drink it regularly after meals. For an even more rewarding tea, add crushed lemongrass and it instantly becomes more fragrant and thirst-quenching. What better way of using up those leftover bits of ginger and lemongrass after making a Thai curry?

Makes a small pot for 4

1 inch fresh ginger root

1 lemongrass stalk

Boiling water

You will also need

Mortar & pestle

Glass infuser or teapot

Tea strainer (if using a teapot)

Put the ginger and the lemongrass in the mortar and crush them with the pestle. Add the crushed aromatics to the heated infuser or pot, fill with boiling water, and let stand for 10 minutes. Then pour the tea and enjoy the fragrances.

Spiced teas & coffee

Adding crushed cardamom seeds to tea is a classic combination in these plants' native Sri Lanka. In the Middle East, cardamom seeds are added to coffee, but try experimenting with vanilla pods, ginger root, cumin, fennel, coriander, and other seeds, or add a pinch or two of ground cinnamon, ginger, or clove to the pot to add an extra zing. Stale tea and coffee never happens in our house, but if you have some lying around, why not try adding spices to the container or to the pot to breathe new life into a brew and create interesting new flavors?

Middle Eastern cardamom coffee

Cardamom has a very distinctive green color and a slightly pungent flavor—warming and pleasing and perfect for spicing teas and coffee. Sri Lanka and India have traded the spice for a thousand years, but of all the Eastern spices, it is probably the least used in Western cooking. Brightly colored cardamoms often feature in the wonderful packs of whole spices that kind friends bring as gifts from their travels. If you don't do a great deal of Indian cooking, flavoring hot drinks is a great way to use them. In the Middle East, coffee and cardamom are boiled together, but it's possible to get a good flavor simply by adding the crushed seeds to coffee before adding boiling water. I find that cardamom imparts a richer, chocolatey taste when used sparingly. If you discover that you really like this combination, add a tablespoon of crushed cardamom seeds to your ground coffee container.

Makes 8 small cups

8 crushed cardamom pods

8 scoops high-roasted ground coffee

Boiling water

Milk or cream, optional

You will also need

Mortar & pestle

Large coffee pot or cafetiere (French press)

Tea strainer, if using a pot

8 small coffee cups

Put the cardamom pods in the mortar and crush them with the pestle. Discard the skin of the pods and crush the seeds lightly. Add the coffee and the crushed cardamom seeds to the heated pot or cafetiere (French press). Add the boiling water, strain and serve immediately in small coffee cups.

Note: This coffee is best served without milk, but you can add milk or cream if you prefer.

Sri Lankan cardamom tea

Makes a pot of tea for 4

4 to 8 cardamom pods, to taste

4 heaped tsp Sri Lankan tea leaves

Boiling water

8 whole cardamom pods for serving

You will also need

Mortar & pestle

Tea strainer

Crush the cardamom pods in the mortar with the pestle, discard the skin of the pod and crush the seeds lightly. Add the tea leaves and crushed cardamom seeds to the heated teapot and pour in the boiling water. Let stand for 10 minutes, then stir well. Put a cardamom pod or 2 into each cup, pour the hot tea through a tea strainer into the cups, and serve at once.

Tangerine & nutmeg hot chocolate

When the weather gets really cold, there is nothing like a cup of homemade hot chocolate to warm and cheer the heart. I have given quantities for one cup, but you can make a potful at a time if you prefer. I use the word "cup" advisedly; this is rich manna from heaven and should be enjoyed a little at a time. I sometimes use tea bowls. I have used dark chocolate; you could use milk or white, but always make it with a quality chocolate. When using a high-percentage cocoa product, the resulting chocolate drink is very dry and needs sweetening. Other chocolate types may not require added sugar.

Makes a small cup, or mug if made with milk before bedtime

3/4 oz dark chocolate (70 to 90% cocoa solids)

1 piece dried tangerine or orange peel

1/2 cup cold water

1 to 2 tsp icing sugar, according to taste and quality of chocolate

For serving

1 to 2 tsp heavy cream

Extra nutmeg

For a bedtime treat add 1/2 cup milk, optional

You will also need

Nutmeg grater

Small skewer or cocktail stick

Put the chocolate and tangerine peel in a nonstick pan. Add the water and gently bring to a simmering on a low heat, stirring to melt the chocolate. Then add sugar to taste, simmer, and stir for 5 to 10 minutes, until the chocolate mixture starts to thicken.

Remove the peel and pour into a small cup or tea bowl and float cream on the top, swirling or marbling using a cocktail stick or small skewer. Sprinkle with a grating of nutmeg.

For a comforting bedtime treat, add the milk to the pan, and once the chocolate has thickened and heated through, pour into a mug and take to bed.

Variation: Try adding a ½ inch piece of vanilla pod and a pinch of ground cinnamon or chili per cup instead of citrus and nutmeg.

Kids' currant tea

Homemade currant jellies make warming drinks for all the family on a cold winter's night. Just add boiling water and stir to dissolve, and add a pinch of spice if you like. Homemade ones are best, but you can also use deli-bought, artisan-made jellies.

Makes 1 mug

2 tsp homemade jelly (see below)

Tiny pinch ground cloves, cinnamon, or nutmeg, optional

Boiling water

You will also need

Heatproof glass mug

Long-handled spoon

Put the jelly in the mug along with the spoon, add a pinch of spice, if using, and top up with boiling water. Stir and enjoy.

Homemade jelly

Makes approx. 1 lb 2 oz

2 lb 3 oz black, red or white currants or berries, or a mixture

Strained juice of 1 lemon

1 cup water

1 cup granulated sugar for every 1 1/4 cup juice

You will also need

Jelly bag

Preserving pan

Jars with lids, washed clean in hot soapy water

Put the fruit in a pan, add the lemon juice and water, and bring slowly to a boil. Cover and cook for 10 to 15 minutes, or until the fruit is soft. Transfer to a jelly bag suspended over a large bowl and leave to drip overnight.

Measure the juice, pour into a clean preserving pan or large, deep saucepan and add the required amount of sugar. Put the pan on a low heat and stir until the sugar has dissolved, then increase the heat and boil for 5 to 10 minutes, until the jelly has reached setting point.

To test whether your mixture is at setting point, remove the pan from the heat, take a teaspoonful of the liquid, put it on a saucer, and leave it in the refrigerator for 5 minutes. After this time, if the jelly wrinkles when you run your finger over the surface, it's ready. If not, put the pan back on the heat, boil for another 5 minutes, and test again.

When ready, if any scum (sugar debris) has formed on the top, skim the jelly using a slotted spoon and pour into the warm, dry jars. Seal and label.

Glossary

Airlock, bubbler, or fermentation lock A simple plastic or glass valve (*see pic* 6, page 106) that allows FERMENTATION gas to bubble out through water or vodka without allowing any air or bacteria back in. In the early stages, when the MUST goes into the FERMENTATION BUCKET, an alternative to fitting an airlock is simply to tip the lid of the bin rather than closing it tightly.

Ascorbic acid A form of vitamin C often added to MUST to stabilize it.

Beer styles Beer comes in a variety of colors, strengths, and styles, broadly divided between ales (those where the yeast migrates to the top once its job is done) and lagers (from German *Lager*, "to store"), where the yeast drops to the floor once FERMENTATION has finished. Refer to *Let Met Tell You About Beer* by Melissa Cole for a full list of beer styles. See also BITTER, IMPERIAL STOUT, PALE ALE, PORTER, STOUT.

Bitter Lightly hopped beer that varies in color from gold to dark amber, and in strength.

Bottles When making beer and cider, it is a good idea to recycle glass beer or cider bottles because they will be strong enough to stand up to the considerable pressures caused by the SECONDARY FERMENTATION during conditioning. You can buy these from homebrew shops, too. Otherwise use plastic with a screwcap. Always use glass with screwcaps, swing-caps, or corks for still wines: clear, green, or brown glass for white wines; green or brown for red wines; clear glass for rosé. Sparkling wines could be bottled in plastic with screwcaps, or in Champagne bottles with corks and ties or cages.

Campden tablet A handy form of metabisulphite used to prevent the growth of mold and bacteria in wines and MUST. One Campden tablet per 1 gallon of wine is added at the start, 24 hours prior to the addition of artificial yeast, and a second tablet after racking, to ensure that fermentation really has stopped.

Citric acid Contained in citrus fruit, in brewing this aids FERMENTATION.

Conditioning or secondary fermentation This process causes beer, cider, or perry to sparkle by absorbing the CO_2 produced by a second FERMENTATION, either in a PRESSURE KEG or a BOTTLE. Once the initial fermentation has finished and the beer has been SIPHONED into a bottle or pressure keg, a small amount of sugar or sugar syrup is added (see box, page 108), before the bottle or keg is sealed tightly. With beer, the bottle or keg should be stored for a couple of days in warm conditions in order to kick off the SECONDARY FERMENTATION, then moved to the coldest place in the house for two weeks to condition. Cider and perry can be bottle-conditioned in the same way.

Crock A traditional earthenware vessel, often used for breadmaking, winemaking, and other drinks that contain yeast.

Demijohn AKA carboy in the USA. Glass vessels of varying capacities, the most usual being 1 gallon. Plastic (PET) demijohns are also available, but I always use glass.

Fermentation In alcoholic drinks, the chemical reaction whereby YEAST converts sugar in the MUST, juice, or WORT into alcohol and carbon dioxide. See also CONDITIONING.

Fermenter or fermentation bucket Deep vessel made from food-grade plastic with a tight-fitting lid, capable of holding an AIRLOCK. These range in size from 1 to 5 gallons. A 2- to 3-gallon container is a useful size unless you want to make large quantities. For the airlock, either buy a lid already modified, or drill the lid and fit with an airlock using a small rubber gasket to seal the joint. If not using an airlock, simply leave the lid ajar. Yeast is added to the MUST or WORT to start off the FERMENTATION process.

Final Gravity See SPECIFIC GRAVITY.

Haze Naturally occurring cloudiness in cider, wine, or beer. Caused by YEASTS and other solids in suspension. With time, this will often "clear" of its own accord.

Hydrometer Like a sugar thermometer, this measures the SPECIFIC GRAVITY, and thus the sugar content, of beer, cider, and wine before and during FERMENTATION (see Note, page 112). For the seasoned winemaker or homebrewer, tables are available to facilitate readings and sugar and alcohol conversions.

Imperial Stout Bigger, bolder, often luxury beer.

Lees Dead YEAST cells and other solid material left after the wine or cider has been RACKED.

Mild A dark, malty, light-tasting British ale.

Must Grape juice or other sugary solution made for FERMENTATION into wine.

Oxidation The effect of exposure to air, causing discoloration and other faults in wine, beer, and cider.

Pale ale Full-bodied, biscuity ale made with pale malt and amber malted barley, with varying levels of hops.

Pectolase Enzyme that breaks down the pectin in wine MUST, which can cause a HAZE to form in some wines.

Porter A lighter form of STOUT.

Pressure barrel, cask, or keg A metal or plastic container capable of containing the pressure caused by SECONDARY FERMENTATION of a new beer. Once the beer is ready, it can be racked off into a pressure barrel with a tap, saving the need to bottle.

Racking The act of SIPHONING beer, cider, or wine out of a FERMENTER or DEMIJOHN into BOTTLES, kegs, or a fresh demijohn, leaving any deposits or LEES behind.

Rousing Stirring the YEAST into MUST, cider, and WORT with a rod or long-handled spoon to give it enough oxygen to get it started.

Secondary fermentation See CONDITIONING.

Siphon A rubber tube used to transfer wine, beer, or cider from one vessel to another. See RACKING.

Sodium metabisulphate See CAMPDEN TABLET.

Specific gravity The relative weight of WORT, MUST, or juice as compared with that of the same volume of water at a given pressure and temperature. This value gives an indication of the sugar available for FERMENTATION, while the final gravity is the amount of sugar left after fermentation. The difference between the two indicates the alcohol by volume (abv) of your drink. (See note, page 112, also HYDROMETER.)

Starter bottle To ensure YEAST can get to work when thrown or "pitched" into the WORT or MUST, sometimes you need to make up a starter culture. Yeast, water, and sugar are mixed in a small bottle and left for an hour so the yeast starts vigorously multiplying before being added to the liquid.

Sterilization See box, page 13.

Stout Dark, bitter beer made with crushed pale malt and chocolate malted barley to give it its characteristic bitterness. Can be dry or sweet.

Sulphiting The addition of metabisulphate to WORT or MUST to STERILIZE the liquids. See CAMPDEN TABLETS.

Tannin An astringent substance from the skins, seeds, and stalks of grapes and other fruit that gives body and finish to wines, cider, and perry.

Tartaric acid (cream of tartar) Naturally occurring in grapes, tartaric acid plays an important role in maintaining the chemical balance of the wine and influencing its taste.

Wort The malt-based, sugar-rich liquid which, when FERMENTED, becomes beer.

Yeast The organism that converts sugar to alcohol is available in a variety of formats for the home drink-maker. You can use either live brewer's yeast or specialist dried yeasts or yeast preparations available from brewing shops. A "wet" yeast from a local brewery will improve the taste of beer. For winemaking there is a huge range of yeasts produced to match the style of wine you want to make (see box, page 84).

Yeast nutrient A specialized blend of nutrients that help YEASTS complete their FERMENTATIONS (see box, page 84).

Directory

CIDER & PERRY

UK

Cider-making courses

Cider & Perry Academy (Peter Mitchell), www.cider-academy.co.uk

The School of Artisan Food www.schoolofartisanfood.org

Everything you need to know

The Cider Workshop, www.ciderworkshop.com; see also the forum www.cider.org.uk/info.htm

The Three Counties Cider & Perry Association, www.thethreecountiesciderandperryassociation.co.uk

South West of England Cidermakers' Association, www.sweca.org.uk

Welsh Perry and Cider Society, www.welshcider.co.uk

Armagh Cider Company, www.armaghcider.com

Pete Brown, www.petebrown.blogspot.com

Bill Bradshaw, www.iamcider.blogspot.com

Buy UK cider & perry

Oliver's Cider and Perry (visit, try & buy) www.oliversciderandperry.co.uk

Once Upon a Tree (visit, try & buy) www.onceuponatree.co.uk

Ross-on-Wye Cider & Perry Company (visit, try, buy & eat) www.rosscider.com

Westons Cider (visit, try, buy, eat & drink) www.westons-cider.co.uk

Bristol Cider Shop (try & buy) www.bristolcidershop.co.uk

The Cider Tap, Euston Tap (try, buy & drink) www.eustontap.com

Truffles Delicatessen (buy in person) www.trufflesdeli.co.uk

Hop Pocket Wine Company (buy in person) www.hoppocketwine.co.uk

Out of the Orchard (Peter Mitchell; buy online) www.outoftheorchard.co.uk

Visit the UK

www.visitherefordshire.co.uk

www.ciderroute.co.uk

www.ciderworkshop.com

www.drinkbritain.com, also breweries

The Cider Museum, www.cidermuseum.co.uk

FRANCE

Normandy Cider

Buy Normandy cider

www.produits-normandie.fr/3-cidre-poire

www.madeinpaysdauge.com/en/bo-cider.html

www.calvados-drouin-boutique.com

www.manoir-de-grandouet.fr, see also www.cellartracker.com/producer.asp?iProducer=115927

Visit Normandy

www.francethisway.com/tourism/normandy-cider-route.php

www.normandie-tourisme.fr

Sleep & eat beautifully with Normandy cider at www.auberge-de-la-source.fr

Eat elegantly with Normandy cider at

www.restaurant-lebreard.com/GB_restaurant_le_breard.php

NORTH AMERICA

Hard Cider

Everything you need to know

Cider & Perry Academy, www.cider-academy.co.uk/usa_scheduled_classes.shtml

www.talisman.com/cider/

Buy North American cider

Poverty Lane Cider www.povertylaneorchards.com

Virtue Cider www.virtuecider.com

Whitewood Cider Co. www.whitewoodcider.com

Visit North America

www.michigan.org/news/cider-mills/

www.visitnewengland.com

BEER

UK

Everything you need to know

Beer Academy, www.beeracademy.co.uk

British Beer and Pub Association, www.beerandpub.com

Campaign for Real Ale (CAMRA) www.camra.org.uk

Northern Ireland, www.camrani.org.uk

Microbreweries Guide Scotland www.microbreweriesguide.com/microbreweriesguide/Welcome.html

Craig Heap (Wales) www.craigheap.wordpress.com/2013/01/13/the-breweries-of-wales-a-full-list

Buy beer in the UK

Teme Valley Brewery www.temevalleybrewery.co.uk

Rhymney Brewery www.rhymneybreweryltd.com

Wye Valley Brewery www.wyevalleybrewery.co.uk

Visit the UK

www.visitabrewery.co.uk

www.visitbritain.com/en/Brewery-tours

NORTH AMERICA & CANADA

Everything you need to know

Brewers Association www.brewersassociation.org/pages/community

Beer Canada, www.beercanada.com

Beer Academy (Canada), www.beeracademy.ca

Buy beer in North America & Canada

www.beermerchants.com

www.thebeerstore.com/beers/canadian

Visit North America & Canada

www.forbes.com/sites/forbestravelguide/2012/02/16/ten-top-american-breweries-worth-a-visit/2/

www.huffingtonpost.ca/2013/10/04/canada-breweries_n_4044818.html

AUSTRALIA

Buy & visit Australian craft beer & cider

www.oakbarrel.com.au

www.southaustralia.com/things-to-do/breweries.aspx

www.tailoredtasmania.com/breweries-distilleries-cider-makers.html

KITS & EQUIPMENT

The Home Brew Shop www.the-home-brew-shop.co.uk

Muntons (UK) www.muntonshomebrew.com; EU, www.brouwland.com/en; North America, www.muntons-inc.com

Vigo, www.vigoltd.com

Young's Home Brew, www.youngshomebrew.co.uk

SOFT DRINKS & JUICE SUPPLIERS

Carey Organic, www.whitethornfarm.co.uk

Jus Single Variety Apple Juice, www.jusapples.co.uk

Belvoir Fruit Farms (pronounced *beaver*), www.belvoirfruitfarms.co.uk
Belvoir elderflower cordial available in the USA, www.thedrinkshop.com

Bottle Green, www.bottlegreendrinks.com

Martinelli's Gold Medal Apple Juices www.martinellis.com

JAR & BOTTLE SUPPLIERS

Kilner, UK (jars & bottles), www.kilnerjar.co.uk

Ampulla (bottles), www.ampulla.co.uk/Shop-For-Glass/c-1-169/

Specialty Bottle, US (bottles) www.specialtybottle.com

Ebottles, Canada (bottles) www.ebottles.com

Pack My Product, Australia (bottles), www.packmyproduct.com.au

Index

Bibliography

Artusi, Pellegrino. *La Scienza in Cucina e l'Arte di Mangiare Bene.* Turin: Giulio Einaudi, 1970.

Beech, FW. *Homemade Wines.* London: Federation of Women's Institutes, 1970.

Beech, FW, and Pollard, A. *Wines and Juices.* London: Hutchinson & Co, 1961.

Beeton, Isabella. *Mrs Beeton's Family Cookery,* New Edition. London: Ward, Lock & Co. Limited, c.1930.

Berry, CJJ. *First Steps in Winemaking.* Hants: Amateur Winemaker Publications Ltd, 1982.

Bullock, Helen. *The Williamsburg Art of Cookery or Accomplished Gentlewoman's Companion.* Williamsburg: Colonial Williamsburg Foundation, 1966.

Chefs of Jim Thompson Restaurants. *At the Table of Jim Thompson.* Singapore: Archipelago Press/Tien Wah Press, 2010.

Cole, Melissa. *Let Met Tell You About Beer.* London: Pavilion Books, 2011.

Della Salda, Anna Gosetti. *Le Ricette Regionali Italiane.* Milan: La Cucina Italiana, 1977.

Farmer, Fannie Merritt. *The Boston Cooking-School Cook Book.* Boston: Little, Brown, and Company, 1923.

Fowles, Gerry. *Winemaking in Style.* Gervin Press, 1992.

Hamilton, Andy. *Booze for Free.* London: Eden Project Books, 2011.

Heaton, Nell, and Simon, André. *Calender of Food & Wine.* London: Faber & Faber Ltd, 1948.

Lea, Andrew. *Craft Cider Making.* Preston: Good Life Press, 2010.

Mattingly, Lilian. *Home Notes Complete Cookery.* London: C. Arthur Pearson Ltd, 1948.

McNulty, Henry. *Vogue Cocktails.* Hong Kong: Mandarin, 1983.

Pradelli, Alessandro Molinari. *Il Grande Libro Della Cucina Veneta.* Rome: Newton and Compton Editori, 2000.

Smith, Eliza. *The Compleat Housewife.* Kings Langley, UK: Arlon House Publishing, 1983.

Tayleur, WHT. *The Penguin Book of Home Brewing and Wine-making.* Middlesex: Penguin, 1982.

Turner, BCA. *Home Winemaking and Brewing.* London: Wolfe Publishing, 1973.

Wheeler, Graham. *Brew Your Own British Real Ale.* St Albans: CAMRA Books, 2009.

Wiesmuller, Maria. *Grappe Aromatiche: Amari e Liquiri.* Kompass, 1996.

Wildsmith, Lindy. *Preserves, Jams, Pickles and Liqueurs.* London: Ryland, Peters & Small, 2004.

Acknowledgments

An author is not enough.
My very special thanks for your help:

Tom Oliver: cider and perry maker *nonpareil*

Peter Mitchell: cider educator and maker

Martin Soble, organic farmer, cider and apple juice producer

Brian Fowler: champion amateur winemaker

Jim and Jean Haines: champion amateur winemakers

Lewis Scott: Cleeve Orchard cider and perry

Guillaume and Christian Drouin: renowned makers of Normandy Calvados, Pommeau, and *cidre*

Lucile and Stephane Grandval: makers of fine Normandy Pommeau and *cidre*

Normandy Tourism

Steve Wood: Poverty Lane Cider, USA

Greg Hall: Virtue Cider, USA

David White: Whitewood Cider Co, USA

Wayne Sosna: Parkers, Ross-on-Wye

Graham Sutton: new product development technologist, Muntons (homebrewing)

Chris Gooch: Theme Valley Brewery

Steve Evans: Rhymney Brewery

Wye Valley Brewery

Vigo Ltd

Without a dedicated and creative team this book would not be half the book it is. Thanks to editors Susanna Forbes and Hilary Lumsden, for keeping me on the straight and narrow; to Cynthia Inions, for supplying fabulous props for us to play with; to photographer Kevin Summers, for his humor and for transforming my imaginings into so many beautiful images; to art director Maggie Town, for mixing the magic and creating the book; to Lydia Halliday for fixing it all together, and to publisher Jacqui Small, for making it happen.

Finally, to my husband, John, and our family and friends, who as usual got a bit of a raw deal while all this was going on.

Useful US & metric conversions

Volume

1 tsp = 5 ml
1 tbsp = 15 ml
1 shot = 1 fl oz = 30 ml
1 cup = 8 fl oz
2 cups = 1 pint
1 pint = 16 fl oz
2 pints = 1 quart
4 quarts = 1 gallon

Weight

1 tsp = 5 g
1 tbsp = 15 g
1 lb = 450 g
2 lb 3 oz = 1 kg